W9-BON-904

What people are saying about Gene Griessman's
The Words Lincoln Lived By:

"A clear and incisive study."

—John Sellers, The Lincoln Curator,
U.S. Library of Congress

"Dr. Gene Griessman has written a work that beautifully captures
the essence of our sixteenth president. Using Lincoln's own words,
the author has skillfully crafted a memorial to Lincoln—not one of
cold granite or marble, but rather a living, breathing testament.
Readers will be inspired by the great wisdom that springs from the
pages of this book."

—Mr. Kim Bauer, Coeditor,
Journal of the Abraham Lincoln Association

"Griessman has done a masterful service in rendering Lincoln's
colossal wisdom of leadership to contemporary leaders and man-
agers. It's uncanny: everything written about leadership today—that
is, anything that's significant—was spoken or written by Lincoln at
least 130 years ago. And Griessman illuminates Lincoln's brilliance
to all of us."

—Warren Bennis, Distinguished Professor of Business
Administration, University of Southern California and author of
Organizing Genius: The Secrets of Creative Collaboration

"Marvelous. *The Words Lincoln Lived By* captures so many truths,
which speak both to us and to future generations."

—Terry Paulson, President,
National Speakers Association

"I love it. A must-read for any serious legal professional."
—John Patrick Dolan, Esq., author of *Negotiate Like the Pros*

"Griessman has captured the heart and mind of the man who changed America for 'good.' You, too, will be changed as you experience Lincoln up close and personal."
— Glenna Salsbury, President, National Speakers Association, author of *The Art of the Fresh Start*

"*First rate.* Lincoln's thoughts on just about anything are compelling, and here, they are artfully broken down into various categories, each brief and brisk. *The Words Lincoln Lived By* makes the quality of his greatness accessible to a wide variety of readers."
— Steve Forbes, Editor-in-Chief, *Forbes* magazine

"Lincoln's words remind us of the values that made America great and that we need now more than ever. His wisdom shines through on every page. This is a book to cherish and share."
— Bill Marriott, CEO, Marriott International, Inc.

"Griessman performs a valuable service in reminding us that Lincoln eloquently championed not only the causes of democracy, freedom, and Union, but also the virtues of self-reliance, industry, ambition, and self-improvement. These are powerful assets for anybody in the race of life."
— Michael Burlingame, author of *The Inner World of Abraham Lincoln*

"An inventive and original compilation—skillfully relating Lincoln's words to the values that give meaning to our lives. Readers will rediscover Lincoln on these pages and appreciate anew his timeless wisdom."
— Harold Holzer, Coeditor, *Lincoln on Democracy*

F

The Words
Lincoln Lived By

52 Timeless Principles to Light Your Path

GENE GRIESSMAN
Winner of the Benjamin Franklin Award

A FIRESIDE BOOK
Published by Simon & Schuster

F

FIRESIDE
Rockefeller Center
1230 Avenue of the Americas
New York, NY 10020

Copyright © 1997 by Gene Griessman

All rights reserved,
including the right of reproduction
in whole or in part in any form.

FIRESIDE and colophon are registered trademarks
of Simon & Schuster Inc.

Designed by Bonni Leon-Berman

Manufactured in the United States of America

7 9 10 8 6

Library of Congress Cataloging-in-Publication Data
Griessman, Gene.
The words Lincoln lived by : 52 timeless principles to light your path /
Gene Griessman.
p. cm.
"A Fireside book."
Includes bibliographical references.
1. Lincoln, Abraham., 1809–1865—Quotations. 2. Conduct of life—Quotations.
3. Quotations, American. I. Lincoln, Abraham, 1809—1865. II. Title.
E.457.99.G84 1998
973.7'092—dc21   97-37317
CIP
ISBN 0-684-84122-3

I must keep some standard of principle fixed within myself.

—ABRAHAM LINCOLN

CONTENTS

INTRODUCTION

When I began studying Abraham Lincoln so that I could write a one-man play based on his life, a rather remarkable transformation began to take place. As I wrote and then enacted his words, I would think deeply about how Lincoln might have responded in various situations. In order to be a good actor, I tried to feel as he felt, speak as he spoke, even breathe as he breathed.

Gradually, I realized that the words of this remarkable man are timeless—particularly those on human nature, democracy, honesty, achievement and disappointment, praise and ridicule, patriotism and idealism. Lincoln himself knew that chosen words can enable you to rise to heights you may now only dream of. Words can paint dreams, correct errors, and pass along truths to the latest generation. Words can interpret the present and speak to the future. Words can stir up the worst or find the best, destroy or build up, tarnish or cleanse.

As I began to incorporate his lessons into my own life, I felt more at peace with myself. I found that I was more persuasive and got along better with others. And I felt more in touch with that Divine Being, without whose assistance Lincoln never could have succeeded.

I learned that whenever I internalized and then acted out great ideas, my life became imbued with a new force. I became more influential in business and in my personal life. Lincoln literally spoke to me from the grave.

Abraham Lincoln was a high achiever of the first rank. His

accomplishments have withstood the most intense historical and literary scrutiny imaginable for well over a century.

Lincoln was not a god, and it is a mistake to try to make him into one. He liked to describe himself as an ordinary man who made the most of himself. A man of great contradictions, he had a temper that caused him problems well into his mature years, but was nevertheless known for his unwillingness to bear a grudge. He could be firm and unyielding on some occasions, yet amazingly flexible and willing to compromise at other times. His mood swings were wild and unpredictable. Seemingly lost in some sad reverie, moments later he might regale visitors with hilarious stories. Although he was a kind and loving father, he chose to be absent from his family for long periods of time, especially during his children's formative years. As a young man, especially, he was anything but refined. But all that changed with time, and the beauty of the Lincoln story is watching him grow in depth of character.

Lincoln became a genuine hero, something much greater than being rich, famous, or powerful. His heroism involved sacrifice, generosity, bravery, and a vision that would transform America. He recognized the great power of *words*, which can produce light in the most unlikely places. Growing up on the frontier in Kentucky, Indiana, and Illinois, Lincoln somehow came in contact with important ideas. They became the propellant that made him the most important leader of his era—and one of the great figures of all time.

Fortunately, we know what many of those ideas are. Lincoln himself left behind an immense written legacy. His contemporaries wrote voluminously about him. After the assassination, his law partner, William H. Herndon, spent the remainder of his life interviewing every person he could find who remembered anything about the sixteenth President.

But ironically, as much as we know about Lincoln, he is still something of a mystery. Though we cannot know everything he thought, we do know enough to start along the path he took to high achievement.

Lincoln used a notebook, which has survived, to use in his famous debates with Stephen Douglas. The very first item, pasted on the inside of the front cover, is the second paragraph of the Declaration of Independence, written by a man he considered his spiritual father—Thomas Jefferson. The words of the Declaration of Independence defined Lincoln, stirred him, and helped make him who he was. He gradually became a master of words himself. In fact, no American President has ever used words more effectively. Some have said that Lincoln used words to "re-invent America."

When he was in his early twenties, a prosperous farmer loaned Lincoln a five-hundred-page copy of the *Revised Laws of Indiana*. Most people would have considered its contents dry as dust, but Lincoln was fascinated by it. It contained the Ordinance of 1787 for the Northwest Territory as well as the Constitution of the United States and the Declaration of Independence.

Throughout the remainder of his life, Lincoln never forgot the ideas embodied in those great documents. He referred to them again and again in his speeches. Years later, when he was invited to the dedication of the military cemetery at Gettysburg, he included an excerpt from the Declaration of Independence in his famous address when he reaffirmed that "all men are created equal."

I have divided this book into fifty-two sections—one for each week of the year. Perhaps you will want to select an entry to read during a quiet moment each week. But you need not read the book in sequence. Simply choose an idea that speaks to you—for example, Diligence or Honesty or Tact. Then reflect on your own life, and perhaps look for opportunities to apply the concept.

The words in this book may change your life. They have already changed mine. Whether you turn to this book as a guide on your path to high achievement, or as a boost to the spirit, or even out of curiosity, I think Abraham Lincoln would be pleased to know that the principles he lived by have the power to illuminate a new generation.

1 . On Determination

*Always bear in mind that
your own resolution to succeed
is more important than any other one thing.*

Lincoln believed failure, like success, comes from within. In his opinion, the ability to succeed depends on the strength of one's own determination. Ironically enough, if anyone had excuses for failure, it was Lincoln. He could have blamed his failures on an unsympathetic and illiterate father, on his lack of schooling, or his ungainly appearance. But Lincoln was not an excuse-maker.

Lincoln's thoughts on determination have a metaphysical flavor. He lived by the principles long taught by great religious teachers and mystics: if you truly want something, you should act as if the object of your desire is already on its way to you. For example, if your goal is to become a lawyer, visualize yourself as a lawyer and you will be well on your way to achieving that dream. Seeing it happen, Lincoln believed, is the way to make it happen. "*Must* is the word," he wrote to a young man who was struggling with schooling. "I know not how to aid you, save in the assurance of one of mature age, and much severe experience, that you *can* not fail, if you resolutely determine, that you *will* not."

Ward Hill Lamon, Lincoln's lawyer friend and confidant,

recalled Lincoln's conviction that he would one day become President: "It seemed to him manifest destiny. 'I will get there,' he would say, seemingly in the fullest confidence of realizing his prediction." And using the power of his own determination, Lincoln was able to make predictions like that one come true.

2 . On Courage

Neither let us be slandered from our duty by false accusations against us, nor frightened from it by menaces of destruction to the Government, nor of dungeons to ourselves. Let us have faith that right makes might; and in that faith, let us, to the end, dare to do our duty, as we understand it.

There are two kinds of courage. One is physical—the kind that shows itself on battlefields. Lincoln felt that he lacked this. He told the painter Francis B. Carpenter that he thought himself a great coward physically and was sure he would make a poor soldier. Yet during the Civil War, he had to bolster the courage of many a weak-kneed general. He stated: "I who am not a specially brave man have had to sustain the sinking courage of these professional fighters in critical times."

The second kind of courage is moral in nature, which Lincoln possessed in abundance. He was able to make tough choices and accept the consequences. Joseph Gillespie, Lincoln's personal friend and fellow lawyer, observed that "he was brave without being rash and never refrained from giving utterance to his views because they were unpopular or likely to bring him into danger."

Courage is what one calls on in spite of fear of danger or fear of failure. Lincoln stated in a speech in 1839: "The *probability* that we may fail in the struggle *ought not* to deter us from the support of a cause we believe to be just; it *shall not* deter me."

3 . On Honesty

I have always wanted to deal with everyone I meet candidly and honestly. If I have made any assertion not warranted by facts, and it is pointed out to me, I will withdraw it cheerfully.

After Lincoln's assassination, a grieving nation began to deify its fallen leader. Glorious stories circulated. Young Abraham may not have chopped down a cherry tree, but he did walk several miles to repay a few pennies he had overcharged a customer. It did not seem to matter much that many of the stories were either exaggerations or outright fabrications. However, enough of the stories were true that long before his death Lincoln earned the name "Honest Abe." A Springfield minister observed: "To call him 'honest Old Abe' is not to my taste but no words can express more correctly the common opinion of him where he is well known."

On the frontier, sporting events often led to disputes and brawls. R. B. Rutledge, the son of the New Salem tavern keeper and brother of Ann Rutledge, remembered that Lincoln was often chosen to resolve controversies. "Mr. Lincoln's judgment was final in all that region of country," Rutledge recalled. "People relied implicitly upon his honesty, integrity, and impartiality."

In Lincoln's day, just as today, lawyers handled the cases of guilty clients—because, of course, under the adversarial system of a democracy, even a guilty person is entitled to the best defense possible. But what is unethical is being dishonest while defending a client. Lincoln was emphatic on this point: "Resolve to be honest at all events," he stated. "If, in your own judgment, you cannot be an honest lawyer, resolve to be honest without being a lawyer. Choose some other occupation, rather than one in the choosing of which you do, in advance, consent to be a knave."

4. On Morality

The true rule, in determining to embrace or reject any thing, is not whether it has any evil in it; but whether it has more of evil than of good. There are few things wholly evil or wholly good. Almost every thing . . . is an inseparable compound of the two; so that our best judgment of the preponderance between them is continually demanded.

Lincoln spent a great deal of time pondering the right course. He believed in a saying that was popular in his day: that one should try to "live up to the light" that one is given.

"Living up to the light" recognizes the limitations of human knowledge. Added light can help us discern right from wrong. In his 1862 Annual Message to Congress, Lincoln urged members to press on "guided by the best light He (the Almighty) gives us."

Lincoln learned, as we all must, that right and wrong are often an "inseparable compound." The moral person stops to evaluate the mix before acting. The Civil War presented many opportunities for Lincoln to do just this. Even before the South fired on Fort Sumter, some advisers had recommended that the slave states be allowed to go their separate ways in peace, sparing over 600,000 lives in the process. But Lincoln felt that his presidential oath "to preserve, protect, and defend the government" was his highest obligation, and one "registered in heaven." Thus he made the painful decision to sacrifice lives in order to preserve the Union. This goal was, as he saw it, a higher good in a dilemma fraught with good and evil.

During the war, a group of clergymen visited the White House to make their views known to the President. One of the ministers commented: "I hope the Lord is on our side." Lincoln replied, "I am not at all concerned about that, for I know that the Lord is *always* on the side of the *right*. But it is my constant anxiety and prayer that I and *this nation* should be on the *Lord's* side."

5 . On Patience

Nothing valuable can be lost by taking time. If there be
an object to hurry any of you, in hot haste, to a step
which you would never take deliberately, that object will be
frustrated by taking time; but no good object
can be frustrated by it.

By temperament, Lincoln was a patient man, capable of bearing long delay and waiting for the right moment. He considered himself a patient man, and must have appeared as such. Charles A. Dana, assistant secretary of war, remembered him as a man who "never was in a hurry, and who never tried to hurry anybody."

Lincoln's inherent patience was due in part to his religious beliefs. On the frontier, preachers debated free will and predestination, a controversy that split churches and denominations. Lincoln favored the predestination doctrine, which formed a framework for his decisions in affairs of state. Friends believed that this philosophy helped him bear his personal misfortunes as well as the agony of the Civil War. "What is to be will be," he sometimes stated, "and no cares of ours can arrest nor reverse the decree."

Lincoln's patience was also due to the practical side of his nature. He had observed as a lawyer and a politician that forcing an issue often spoiled a desired outcome. He came to the conclusion that political and legal processes, like flowers and trees, followed a natural sequence of development. Using an analogy from agriculture, Lincoln observed: "A man watches his pear-tree day after day, impatient for the ripening of the fruit. Let him attempt to *force* the process, and he may spoil both fruit and tree. But let him patiently *wait*, and the ripe pear at length falls into his lap!"

6. On Magnanimity

With malice toward none . . .

Leaders in times of war typically try to dehumanize their opponents. But Lincoln was not a typical leader. He is celebrated for the humane manner in which he portrayed his foes—during one of the bloodiest wars in history. The Gospel admonition "Bless them that curse you" was one of the principles he lived by.

"He was certainly a very poor hater," longtime friend Leonard Swett remembered. Joseph Gillespie agreed: "He never manifested any bitter hatred towards his enemies. It was enough for him in a controversy to get the better of his adversary in argument without descending to personal abuse."

During the Civil War, no man was hated more than Lincoln. He was called a gorilla, a beast, a blood-thirsty tyrant. In the South, they sang derisive songs about him. "Jeff Davis rides a snow white horse; Abe Lincoln rides a mule. Jeff Davis is a gentleman; Abe Lincoln is a fool." And that was one of the milder ones.

Lincoln did not return the feelings in kind. Hours before his assassination, Lincoln met with his cabinet to discuss what should be done to Confederate leaders. Should they be tried as traitors and hanged? Lincoln replied: "I hope there will be no persecution, no bloody work after the war is over. None need expect me to take part in hanging or killing them. Enough lives have been sacrificed. We must extinguish our resentment if we expect harmony and union."

News of Lincoln's magnanimity spread abroad. The *Spectator* in London compared him to two great British leaders, John Hampden and Oliver Cromwell, observing, "His gentleness and generosity of feeling toward his foes are almost greater than we should expect from either of them."

7 . On Time Management

*This habit of uselessly wasting time is the whole difficulty;
and it is vastly important . . . that you should break
this habit.*

According to teachers and ministers in Lincoln's time, it was imperative to make the most of every moment. Idleness was dangerous because it could lead to other vices. Old proverbs concurred: "An idle brain is the devil's workshop"; "An idle person tempts the devil to tempt him"; "Sloth is the devil's pillow." If idleness is turned into a habit, the theory went, the results could be disastrous. Habits plow a furrow in the mind. The harvest of a person's lifetime depends on what those furrows are like, how deep they are, and what is sown in them.

An early acquaintance remembered the first time he saw Lincoln with his stepbrother, John Johnston. The man said he would have picked talkative, outgoing Johnston to become the success. However, Lincoln's career was marked by steady growth, while Johnston could never get his life together.

Lincoln knew his stepbrother was an idler and urged him to do something about it: "Your thousand pretences for not getting along better are all nonsense," Lincoln wrote. "They deceive nobody but yourself. . . . *Face* the truth—which truth is, you are destitute because you have *idled* away all your time."

Johnston eventually sold the little land he owned and

moved to Arkansas, hoping to find fortune there. Unfortunately, he carried his habits with him and he returned to Illinois within a year. When he died a year later, a defeated man, his personal property was valued at $55.90.

8 . On Work

The mode is very simple, though laborious and tedious. It is only to get the books, and read, and study them carefully . . . Work, work, work is the main thing.

During the Civil War, Lincoln wrote the following letter of recommendation to the commander of the Washington arsenal: "My dear Sir: The lady—bearer of this—says she has two sons who want to work. Set them at it, if possible. Wanting to work is so rare a merit, that it should be encouraged. Yours truly, A. Lincoln."

Lincoln's father, Thomas Lincoln, would probably have been surprised to hear his son recommending hard work. His father saw Abraham as an idler who preferred reading to physical labor. Because his narrow conception of work did not include intellectual labor, Thomas had misread his son. Later the son joked to a friend that his father taught him to work, but he never taught him to love it.

Ironically enough, Lincoln actually did perform a fair amount of manual labor felling trees, splitting rails, digging potatoes, and working on boats and rafts. But it was hard work for small pay. And as soon as he could, Lincoln turned his energies to labor that, while different, was just as demanding: studying, visualizing, conceptualizing, problem-solving, and planning.

9 . On Diligence

Half finished work generally proves to be labor lost. . . .

No other principle comes closer to accounting for Lincoln's success than diligence. Those who are diligent work steadily. They pay unremitting attention to the task at hand. They are careful. Still, diligence encompasses more than just work. It involves *how* a person works. It was a term with which Lincoln became familiar in his childhood reading. Idleness and sloth are dangerous vices, he read, but diligence is a great virtue.

As an ambitious young man, Lincoln would note that diligence was viewed as a key to success. "See'st thou a man diligent in his business," one Bible proverb observed. "He shall stand before kings, and not before mean men." These lines, Lincoln learned, were the personal motto of the famed Benjamin Franklin.

Like Franklin, Lincoln's diligence and mindfulness became legendary. The care that Lincoln consistently applied to his work can be seen even in his handwriting. Researchers have discovered thousands of meticulously written legal documents filed away in dusty courthouse drawers.

In notes he prepared for lawyers, Lincoln recommended forming the habit of diligence: "The leading rule for the lawyer, as for the man of every calling, is *diligence*. Leave nothing for to-morrow, which can be done to-day. Never let your correspondence fall behind. Whatever piece of business you have in hand, before stopping, do all the labor pertaining to it which can *then* be done."

Evidently, Lincoln practiced the habit that he prescribed. Henry J. Raymond, who was the editor of the *New York Times* during Lincoln's presidency, observed that Lincoln brought with him to Washington the habits that had worked so well in his law practice: "He brought to every question—the loftiest and most imposing—the same patient inquiry into details, the same eager longing to know and do exactly what was just and right, and the same working-day, plodding, laborious devotion, which characterized his management of a client's case in Springfield."

10. On Curiosity

I know of nothing so pleasant to the mind, as the discovery of anything that is at once new and valuable.

Lincoln was known for his profound curiosity. He believed in the power of facts, and had neither faith nor respect for "say-so's," whether they came from old traditions or venerable authorities. He tested everything. According to William Herndon, clocks, paddle wheels, engines, inventions of all sorts, language, words and expressions—all fascinated Lincoln. He wanted to know where they came from and how they worked, both "inside and outside, upside and downside. He would stop in the street to study a machine. He would whittle a thing to a point, and then count the numberless inclined planes and their pitch making the point."

Lincoln would have made a fine scientist. "Every blade of grass is a study," he told the Wisconsin State Agricultural Society. He certainly had the temperament for scientific investigation. "All creation is a mine," Lincoln observed in a lecture he gave on discoveries and inventions, "and every man, a miner." Joshua Speed wrote: "Lincoln studied and appropriated to himself all that came within his observation. Everything that he saw, read, or heard added to the store of his information—because he thought upon it. No truth was too small to escape his observation, and no problem too intricate to escape a solution, if it was capable of being solved."

11. On Vision

*If we could first know where we are, and whither we are
tending, we could then better judge what to do,
and how to do it.*

Great leaders are visionary thinkers. They envision a future
that can be achieved and they communicate this vision to their
followers. Though they cannot always control events, they can
still interpret them and help their followers understand what is
happening around them.

Lincoln's skill as a visionary was profound. "I can see that
time [the extermination of slavery] is coming—whoever can
wait for it will see it—whoever stands in its way will be run over
by it," he told Leonard Swett in 1863. He realized that a slave
society and a free society are incompatible and could not coexist forever. In his memorable "House Divided" speech (see p.
117) he predicted that the nation would eventually become one
or the other—a statement that many believed cost him his Senate bid. When they told him so, Lincoln replied: "Gentlemen,
you may think that speech was a mistake, but I never have
believed it was, and you will see the day when you will consider
it was the wisest thing I ever said."

Lincoln called for expanded rights for women long before
the triumph of the women's suffrage movement. William Herndon recalled: "Mr. Lincoln as early as 1836 issued a political

handbill in which he declared himself for women's rights. His keen sense of justice could not refuse woman the rights which he demanded for himself, [and he] said to me often that that question was one of time only."

In order to understand the world around him, Lincoln relied mainly on close observation and the relation between cause and effect. "There were no accidents in his philosophy," Herndon wrote. "Every effect had its cause." Once Lincoln had a sense of where events were moving, he positioned himself so to take advantage of the movement. His friend Leonard Swett observed: "His tactics were to get himself in the right place and remain there still, until events would find him in that place."

12. On Assertiveness

You must not wait to be brought forward by
the older men. . . . Do you suppose that
I should ever have got into notice if
I had waited to be hunted up
and pushed forward by older men?

"The man who thinks Lincoln calmly sat down and gathered his robes around him, waiting for the people to call him, has a very erroneous knowledge of Lincoln," Herndon wrote. He portrayed Lincoln as an assertive man who was always thinking ahead and trying to position himself to obtain an ever more ambitious level in his career. He ran for office the first time when he was twenty-three years old and, although he was defeated, came back to win four straight terms in the Illinois legislature. Years later, as a result of these experiences, he advised young men with the words above.

When war came, Lincoln looked for military leaders who were as assertive as he was. He found an answer in Ulysses S. Grant, a general who had experienced stunning successes at Fort Henry and Fort Donelson. But when Grant met with near disaster at Shiloh, he became enormously unpopular with the public. A journalist, A. K. McClure, was with Lincoln when he decided Grant's fate: "He sat before the open fire in the old Cabinet room, most of the time with his feet up on the high marble mantel. . . . Lincoln remained silent for what seemed a very long time. He then gathered himself up in his chair and said in a tone of earnestness that I shall never forget: '*I can't spare this man; he fights.*'"

The charismatic but overly cautious commander of the Army of the Potomac, General George McClellan, was another matter. Lincoln employed one tactic after another to get McClellan to take the initiative, all to no avail. "You are probably engaged with the enemy," he observed in one dispatch, adding wryly: "I suppose he made the attack." Feeling intense pressure to fire McClellan, Lincoln entreated him like a father: "It is indispensable to *you* that you strike a blow . . . I have never written you, or spoken to you, in greater kindness of feeling than now, nor with a fuller purpose to sustain you, so far as in my most anxious judgment, I consistently can. *But you must act.*"

13. On Tenacity

I expect to maintain this contest until successful, or till I die, or am conquered, or my term expires, or Congress or the country forsakes me.

Lincoln believed that sticking to a decision, once made, would strengthen the individual. He saw the human will as a muscle that becomes powerful through exercise, but can become flabby and weak through lack of use.

In the wake of horribly high casualties the Union Army had suffered at Cold Harbor and Petersburg, Lincoln sent the following message to Ulysses S. Grant: "I have seen your dispatch expressing your unwillingness to break your hold where you are. Neither am I willing. Hold on with a bull-dog grip, and chew and choke as much as possible." They were admirable words, given the severity of the situation. For months the Army of the Potomac had been repulsed, and seemed to be going nowhere. Criticism of Lincoln's administration had reached crescendo pitch. But instead of resignedly yielding to the pressures, Lincoln continued to support his general, look for new strategies, and remain doggedly resolute.

"I must save this government if possible," he stated. "What I *cannot* do, of course I *will* not do; but it may as well be understood, once for all, that I shall not surrender this game leaving any available card unplayed." He urged Congress to break with old traditions in order to achieve its goals. "The dogmas of the quiet past are inadequate to the stormy present," he stated. "As our case is new, so we must think anew, and act anew. We must disenthrall ourselves, and then we shall save our country."

During those dark days, he wrote an inspiring and supportive letter to a discouraged West Point cadet. His words demonstrate the depth of his own tenacity, which would ultimately make victory possible: "Adhere to your purpose and you will soon feel as well as you ever did. On the contrary, if you falter, and give up, you will lose the power of keeping any resolution, and will regret it all your life. . . . Stick to your purpose."

1 4 . On Self-Preservation

I have found that when one is embarrassed,
usually the shortest way to get through with it
is to quit talking about it or thinking about it,
and go at something else.

Lincoln certainly had his share of unhappy experiences. Often, they plunged him into depression so severe that his friends feared for him. Gradually, though, he discovered what to do when he was rejected, belittled, or attacked. He taught himself to view failures as experiences to learn from instead of disasters to be brooded over. He learned when to stop worrying and move on to something else.

He also would retreat within himself, using the withdrawal period to regroup his powers. His secretary John G. Nicolay observed that when official business had ended, the President would shut the door and "would sometimes sit for an hour in complete silence, his eyes almost shut, the inner man apparently as far from him as if the form in the chair were a petrified image." By looking inward, he found the strength to continue. Midway through the Civil War, he told a large delegation: "I shall always try and preserve one friend within me, who never fails me, to tell me that . . . I have acted right."

On some occasions he would tell a funny story. "I laugh because I must not weep—that's all, that's all," he said of himself. "A funny story, if it has the element of genuine wit . . . puts new life into me." Sometimes, if an individual had upset him and he wanted to work out his feelings, he would write the man a letter that he never intended to mail. Noting this psychological tactic, the famed Civil War historian and novelist Shelby Foote concluded, "Lincoln was his own psychiatrist."

Perhaps most important was Lincoln's growing ability to validate himself. He had no desperate need for others' praise to be self-confident. That knowledge came from within.

15. On Justice

The severest justice may not always be the best policy.

Lincoln was a kind man, full of sympathy and humaneness, and he knew justice must be tempered with compassion. The challenge was to find the right balance. Kindness, if not grounded in fundamental principles of right and wrong, can become mere sentimentality, and Lincoln had learned that personal kindness must sometimes be sublimated to considerations of the law and the larger good of the community. He had been in many courtroom situations where feelings of sympathy had to be balanced with the demands of justice. Justice without cruelty was his goal. As his old roommate Joshua Speed stated, "He carried from his home on the prairies to Washington the same gentleness of disposition and kindness of heart." But also, as his friend and chronicler Herndon wrote, "He held his heart subject to his head and conscience. His humanity had to defer to his sense of justice and the eternal right."

The Civil War brought a bitter irony to Lincoln's life that the President often reflected upon. Although he shuddered at even killing an animal, as commander in chief he was responsible for sending thousands of young men to violent deaths. Nevertheless, because he believed it was essential to preserve the Union, he refused to make peace. But he did try to save lives where possible. Over the protests of his secretary of war and numerous officers who complained that the President was destroying military discipline, Lincoln often held up the paper-work of soldiers sentenced to be shot. He also revoked the death sentence for soldiers penalized for sleeping on duty or desertion. At least, he reasoned, he could save a few.

16. On Influence

*If you would win a man to your cause, first convince him that
you are his sincere friend. Therein is a drop of honey that
catches his heart, which . . . when once gained,
you will find but little trouble in convincing his judgment
of the justice of your cause.*

Good-hearted, gentle persuasion was always Lincoln's way.
During his great debates with Douglas, a correspondent for the
New York Tribune wrote that "Lincoln is colloquial, affable,
good-natured, almost jolly. He states the case at issue with so
much easy good humor and fairness that his opponents are
almost persuaded he is not an opponent at all."

Lincoln's dealings with leaders of the temperance movement provide a good example of his overall approach to people
with different ideas or lifestyles. Though he sometimes spoke at
temperance meetings, Lincoln did not agree with the movement's heavy-handed tactics: ridiculing alcoholics, abusing bar-
tenders, and sometimes even physical violence. Persuade, he
advised. Don't ridicule or humiliate if you wish to change people's behavior. They must be convinced that you have their best
interests at heart. "When the conduct of men is designed to be
influenced," Lincoln told a gathering of the Washington Temperance Society of Springfield, "*persuasion*, kind, unassuming
persuasion, should ever be adopted."

1 7 . On Responsibility

I am here; I must do the best I can, and bear the responsibility of taking the course which I feel I ought to take.

Only leaders of the highest integrity will take responsibility for plans that do not succeed. Lincoln was such a leader. He shouldered the blame during the long, dangerous years of the Civil War when his advisers bickered, his generals blundered, and Union forces suffered one disastrous defeat after another. However, whenever his men were successful, he gave them the credit. The battle of Gettysburg provides a telling example. Soon after the fighting ended, Lincoln sent General George Meade this message: "You will follow up and attack General Lee as soon as possible before he can cross the river. If you fail this dispatch will clear you from all responsibility, and if you succeed, you may destroy it." As it turned out, Meade delayed, Lee's troops escaped as Lincoln had predicted, and the war was prolonged many months. Lincoln wrote a sad letter of reprimand to Meade but never sent it. The letter was found among Lincoln's papers after his death.

Lincoln understood that his position gave him some responsibilities that could not be evaded or delegated. In no uncertain language, he reminded General Grant not to infringe on his own presidential responsibilities: "You are not to decide, discuss, or confer upon any political question. Such questions the President holds in his own hands, and will submit them to no military conferences or conventions." And when some of his cabinet members criticized him, Lincoln responded humbly but assertively: "I don't know but that God has created some one man great enough to comprehend the whole of this stupendous crisis and transaction from beginning to end, and endowed him with sufficient wisdom to manage and direct it. I confess I do not fully understand, and foresee it all. But I am placed here where I am obliged to the best of my poor ability to deal with it."

The responsibilities of leadership are not always profound. Many American presidents have served in relatively tranquil times. Not Lincoln. He understood and accepted the challenge of leading a vast country through some of its most momentous and troublesome times. "Fellow-citizens, *we* cannot escape history," Lincoln told Congress in 1862. "We of this Congress and this administration, will be remembered in spite of ourselves. No personal significance, or insignificance, can spare one or another of us. The fiery trial through which we pass, will light us down, in honor or dishonor, to the latest generation." (See p. 119.)

18. On Communication

I determined to be so clear that no honest man could misunderstand me and no dishonest one could successfully misrepresent me.

Lincoln was a master communicator. He was effective with small and large groups, either one-on-one or from the platform. His strength lay in explaining complex ideas accurately and clearly. "Don't shoot too high—aim lower and the common people will understand you," he advised William Herndon. "They are the ones you want to reach—at least they are the ones you ought to reach. The educated and refined people will understand you any way. If you aim too high your ideas will go over the head of the masses, and only hit those who need no hitting."

Lincoln deliberately chose illustrations and words that ordinary people could understand. After he became President, he decided to use the word "sugar-coated" in one of his official statements. The public printer respectfully suggested that the President choose a more refined expression. Lincoln replied: "That term expresses precisely my idea, and I am not going to change it. The time will never come in this country when the people will not understand exactly what 'sugar-coated' means."

Content as well as diction made Lincoln an effective communicator. "He carefully studied and thought out the best way of saying everything as well as the substance of what he should say," a contemporary commented. This meant taking into account who his audience was and how much they could understand. Harriet Beecher Stowe said of him, "His rejection of what is called fine writing was as deliberate as St. Paul's, and for the same reason—because he felt that he was speaking on a subject which must be made clear to the lowest intellect."

Examples and little stories became the hallmark of Lincoln's communication style. "He was the most rigidly logical in debate and yet he illustrated every point by a humorous anecdote," recalled his friend Joseph Gillespie. It was a deliberately planned strategy. "Common people . . . are more easily influenced and informed through the medium of a broad illustration than in any other way," he once commented. "As to what the hypercritical few may think, I don't care."

19. On Focus

I know that general reading broadens the mind—makes it universal, but it never makes a precise deep clear mind.

Lincoln preferred depth to breadth. He felt that if an individual is too broad in his or her knowledge—too versatile—then that knowledge may in fact be shallow. He believed that general reading—as opposed to targeted reading—can become an addiction that saps intellectual energy. He had no time for dilettantes, and realized that the world's greatest achievers were totally immersed in their respective subjects.

In his quest to gain deep knowledge, Lincoln sought out the finest teachers available. When asked to try a patent-infringement case, he found the most skilled architect in town and asked him to become a partner: "I know nothing about mechanics—never made it a study," he told him. "I want you to make a list of the best works . . . I will furnish the money, and you can send to Chicago or New York for them. I want you to come to my house one night each week and give me instruction." The architect did just that and Lincoln won the case. In fact, Lincoln gained such a reputation that he became known as the best attorney to retain for patent-right cases brought into the Illinois Supreme Court.

When he was President, his cabinet was made up of some of the nation's most gifted individuals. One of them, William Henry Seward from New York, had been both his state's governor and U.S. senator. A college graduate who had traveled extensively, Seward had experience that Lincoln lacked.

Lincoln responded to Seward's superior knowledge by asking for instruction. Many a Sunday, Seward would come over to the White House at the President's invitation to tutor him. It was this kind of tactic that enabled a man with less than a year's schooling to survive as the leader of the nation. He believed he could learn anything he needed to know.

20. On Compromise

The spirit of concession and compromise—that spirit which has never failed us in past perils . . . may be safely trusted for all the future.

While Lincoln's strength of character and principle were unshakable, he was nonetheless a first-rate compromiser. Harriet Beecher Stowe once observed that "Lincoln's whole nature inclined him to be a harmonizer of conflicting parties rather than a committed combatant on either side."

Lincoln understood that compromise is necessary in everyday life. His experience as a lawyer in some five thousand cases taught him that often half a loaf is better than no loaf at all. "Persuade your neighbors to compromise whenever you can," he wrote in a lecture for lawyers. "Point out to them how the *nominal* winner is often a *real* loser—in fees, and expenses, and waste of time." He also knew that compromise is essential in government. As a state legislator, Lincoln acquired the ability to deal with individuals who had widely different interests, motives, and agendas. He came to the presidency as a compromise candidate: at the Republican convention, Lincoln was the first choice of only a few, but the second choice of many. He didn't win the nomination until the supporters of the front-runners faltered.

As a wartime President, Lincoln worked out one compromise after another to hold the nation together until victory could be achieved. He helped forge an unlikely coalition of pro-Union slaveholders, abolitionists, conservatives, moderates, and radicals. He once commented that he had a gift for keeping discordant individuals and groups together. Lincoln achieved his most important goals by understanding the power of compromise.

21. On Flexibility

I shall try to correct errors when shown to be errors; and I shall adopt new views so fast as they shall appear to be true views.

Critics accused Lincoln of being a wishy-washy President. He seemed to hesitate when bold action was called for. He appeared to procrastinate. To many, including publisher Horace Greeley, he looked like an unsteady President, utterly lacking a driving policy. Greeley regularly printed highly unflattering articles about the President, one of which Lincoln eventually answered with the words above.

If convincing new evidence appeared, Lincoln *would* change his position, even break a promise. Many people sincerely believe that promises must always be kept, no matter what. Not Lincoln. "Bad promises are better broken than kept," he stated—if keeping the bad promise is "adverse to the public interest."

On one occasion, a friend of Lincoln's came into the room while the President was being shaved. The two chatted about several matters, and then the visitor commented, "Mr. Lincoln, if anybody had told me that in a general crisis like this the people were going out to a little one-horse town to pick out a one-horse lawyer for President, I wouldn't have believed it."

Lincoln's response was so vigorous that at first his friend

thought he was angry. Whirling about in his chair, his face white with lather, the President swept the barber aside and answered. "Neither would I; but it was a time when a man with a policy would have been fatal to the country. I have never had a policy; I have simply tried to do what seemed best each day as each day came."

22. On Simplicity

Common looking people are the best in the world: that is the reason the Lord makes so many of them.

Certain self-made men become pompous or inaccessible with the advent of power or wealth. Not Lincoln. Judge David Davis, who had known Lincoln as a young lawyer, described him as "the most simple and unostentatious of men in his habits, having few wants, and those easily supplied." *New York Times* editor Henry J. Raymond observed that the most striking characteristic of Lincoln's personal demeanor was his "utter unconsciousness of his position."

Lincoln usually referred to himself as "Lincoln" or sometimes as the "Chief Magistrate of the People." It is true that some individuals addressed him as "Your Excellency," and he did not object; but he unceremoniously called his office "this place" or "the shop." When an acquaintance called him "Mr. President," Lincoln stopped him: "Call me Lincoln. 'Mr. President' is entirely too formal for us." On one occasion when he was treated rather brusquely, he chuckled that there was "no smell of royalty" about his presidency.

As a congressman, his attitude was similar. "Suppose you do not prefix the 'Hon.' to the address on your letters to me any more," he wrote to his wife. "I like the letters very much, but I would rather they should not have that upon them."

Lincoln's appearance and style of dressing also reflected

his lack of pretension. With the possible exception of his hat, his clothing was restrained. Though the hat almost became a caricature, he found it a handy place in which to store letters and notes. When he ran for President, a young girl, Grace Bedell, suggested that he grow a beard, which she believed would improve his chances for election. Lincoln sent her a little note with these words: "As to the whiskers, having never worn any, do you not think people would call it a piece of silly affect[at]ion if I were to begin it now?" But a month later, he set aside his concerns and followed her advice.

"In my life I have seen a good number of men distinguished by their talents or their station," wrote London journalist Edward Dicey, "but I never saw any one, so apparently unconscious that this distinction conferred upon him any superiority, as Abraham Lincoln."

23. On Energy

*I don't like to hear cut-and-dried sermons. No—when I
hear a man preach, I like to see him act
as if he were fighting bees.*

In a demanding environment where dull orators could lose their
audience—and thus the chance to communicate their message—Lincoln became known as the best stump speaker of the
West. Why? Because of his enormous fervor and enthusiasm
coupled with wit and logic. When he delivered what has become
known as the "lost speech" in 1856, one observer remembered:
"I have never heard such a speech before or since. He would
raise his great arm, with clenched fist above his head, and shake
it in the air and bring it down with an emphasis that fairly
made your hair stand on end and your heart quit beating."
The journalist from the *Chicago Tribune* who had come to cover
the event wrote a few sentences, but then got so caught up in the
excitement that he laid down his pencil. No authentic record has
ever been found of all Lincoln said that day.

Lincoln was set apart by his ability to combine energy with
mathematically precise logic. During one of his speeches,
Herndon captured this approach: "The smothered flame broke
out; enthusiasm unusual to him blazed up; his eyes were aglow
with an inspiration. . . . His speech was full of fire and energy
and force; it was logic; it was pathos; it was enthusiasm; it was

justice, equity, truth, and right set ablaze by the divine fires of a soul maddened by the wrong; it was hard, heavy, knotty, gnarly, backed with wrath." It was logic set on fire that helped to make Lincoln the stunning national figure we admire today.

24. On Tact

The sharpness of a refusal or the edge of a rebuke may be blunted by an appropriate story, so as to save wounding feeling and yet serve the purpose.

All serious Lincoln scholars agree that Lincoln became the most tactful of men. J. G. Randall, one of the greatest Lincoln scholars, called the President's manner "kindness skillfully extended—the opposite of brusqueness, clumsiness, or impulsive blurting out of one's feelings." The youthful Lincoln was often anything but tactful, especially in his attacks on political opponents. Gradually, he learned to reach a person indirectly rather than by frontal attack.

"His tact was remarkable," fellow lawyer Abram Bergen remembered. "He carefully studied and thought out the best way of saying everything, as well as the substance of what he should say." Lincoln learned to use tactics that were appropriate to each individual. He could turn away an opponent's wrath with just the right word, anecdote, or action, and had a remarkable capacity to imagine himself in the other person's place. This gave him the ability to predict what the other person was likely to do, and to formulate an appropriate strategy.

During the Civil War, an angry governor traveled to Washington to complain about the way the draft was being administered in his state. After a stormy meeting with the secretary of war, the governor demanded to see the President. James B.

Fry, then the provost-marshal-general in charge of army recruitment, remembered waiting anxiously, expecting any moment to be summoned to the White House. Instead of further conflict, however, the governor eventually returned with a pleasant smile to say goodbye. When Fry saw the President, he asked if he had to make big concessions to the governor. "Oh, no," Lincoln replied, "I did not concede anything. You know how that Illinois farmer managed the big log that lay in the middle of his field! It was too big to haul out, too knotty to split, and too wet and soggy to burn. *'I ploughed around it,'* said the farmer." Lincoln explained, "That's the way I got rid of Governor ———. *I ploughed around him,* but it took me three mortal hours to do it."

25. On Conciliation

*No man [who has] resolved to make the most of himself
can spare time for personal contention.*

Perhaps the most important lesson Lincoln ever learned was to
avoid personal quarrels. As a practicing attorney, he was constantly involved in disputes. And as a politician, he regularly
engaged in highly partisan struggles. The lesson Lincoln had to
learn was to disagree without being disagreeable, to argue in
such a way that an opponent did not become an enemy.

It was a lesson that Lincoln did not learn easily. His one-
time law partner Stephen T. Logan remembered that Lincoln
had a "very high temper" when aroused. "He controlled it then
in a general way, though it would break out sometimes—and at
those times it didn't take much to make him whip a man."

As a young politician, he taunted opponents, sometimes
calling them fools, liars, and thieves. He wrote vicious satires,
occasionally anonymously. One letter even led to a duel with a
politician named James Shields. The two men actually met
with broadswords. At the last minute their seconds intervened.

Somehow, Lincoln outgrew the habit of quarreling. Perhaps it was the aborted duel with Shields that became a lifelong
source of embarrassment to Lincoln. By the time he reached
the White House, his quarreling days were far behind him. "A
man has not the time to spend half his life in quarrels," he was

able to state with sincerity. Lincoln illustrated the lesson with an example. "Better give your path to a dog than be bitten by him in contesting for the right. Even killing the dog [will] not cure the bite."

26. On Forgiveness

*I am a patient man—always willing to forgive on the
Christian terms of repentance, and also to give ample time
for repentance.*

Over the course of his life, Lincoln developed the ability to rise
above personal resentment, to forgive and to forget. He came to
the conclusion that time and energy devoted to getting even is
better spent getting ahead. "There may sometimes be ungener-
ous attempts to keep a young man down," he once commented,
"and they will succeed, too, if he allows his mind to be diverted
from its true channel to brood over the attempted injury."

Lincoln said that when "any man ceases to attack me, I
never remember the past against him." And he was as good as
his word. In 1855, Lincoln traveled to Cincinnati to participate
in a patent-infringement case with one Edwin Stanton, who
had become a highly successful attorney in Pittsburgh. Stanton
treated Lincoln in a shamelessly rude manner. "Why did you
bring that damned long-armed Ape here?" he asked the team's
lead attorney. "He does not know anything and can do you no
good." Stanton never conferred with Lincoln, never invited
him to his table or his room, never walked to and from the court
with him, even though they stayed at the same hotel and were in
court together for a week. Seven years later, President Lincoln
chose Stanton as his secretary of war.

On the eve of Lincoln's election to a second presidential term, a group gathered to celebrate. Several individuals commented nastily about certain politicians who had not supported the President. Lincoln responded this way: "You have more of that feeling of personal resentment than I have. Perhaps I have too little of it; but I never thought it paid."

27. On Ambition

I'll study and get ready, and then the chance will come.

Josiah Crawford was an Indiana farmer who hired Lincoln to shuck corn and daub his cabin in the 1820s. Young Lincoln told Josiah's wife Elizabeth: "I don't always intend to delve, grub, shuck corn, split rails and the like." According to Ward Hill Lamon, Lincoln had dreamed of becoming President since he was a young boy. Lamon concluded: "Ambition was one of the ruling characteristics of this great man from the cradle to the grave."

Lincoln believed he was destined for great things, and it was his responsibility to get ready for them. "He was always calculating, and always planning ahead," Herndon wrote. "His ambition was a little engine that knew no rest."

Every job Lincoln took gave him an opportunity to prepare. As a surveyor, he learned to be meticulous and to deal with neighbors' disputes over boundary lines in a fair and diplomatic manner. As postmaster, he read newspapers before delivering them. Working at the grocery and mill in New Salem, Lincoln built up a political constituency. But it was as a lawyer that he found a certain path for his ascent.

Though Lincoln was restlessly ambitious, it was not derived from lust for personal wealth or power. "He was unquestionably ambitious for official distinction," Joseph Gillespie said of him, "but he only desired place to enable him to do good and serve his country and his kind."

28. On Study

*A capacity, and taste, for reading gives access to whatever has
already been discovered by others. It is the key, or one
of the keys, to the already solved problems. And not only so.
It gives a relish, and facility, for successfully
pursuing the unsolved ones.*

On the frontier, there simply were not many books available. At
first, young Lincoln read and studied whatever he could find:
the Bible, *Aesop's Fables, Pilgrim's Progress*, and Weems's *Life
of Washington.* He walked six miles to borrow a copy of
Kirkham's *English Grammar* because Mentor Graham, the
schoolteacher in New Salem, told him anyone in the public eye
should know grammar. He also studied Murray's *English
Reader*, where he found excerpts from Pliny, Heraclitus,
Cicero, Addison, Goldsmith, and Locke as well as an essay by
Quintus Curtius on slavery.

He acquired Blackstone's *Commentaries*—a classic of the
legal profession. "Never in my whole life was my mind so thoroughly absorbed," Lincoln later recalled. "I read until I
devoured them."

He often carried a book with him in his rambles through
the woods and walks by the Sangamon River. Sometimes he
would go to the cooper's shop and build a fire with the waste
wood lying about so he could read by the flickering light. "His
practice was when he wished to indelibly fix anything he was

reading or studying on his mind to write it down," Robert B. Rutledge recalled. "[I] have known him to write whole pages of books he was reading." When he was clerking in the store, Lincoln would open his book—if only for five minutes at a time—stop to serve the occasional customer who walked in, and then go back to his studies.

Even after he had achieved his ultimate goal—the presidency—Lincoln never lost his thirst for knowledge. After his inauguration, he applied his old habit to new resources, this time in the Library of Congress, where he devoured books on military strategy. He was following a principle that had served him well throughout life. "Get the books and read and study them in their principal features; and that is the main thing," he wrote an aspiring lawyer. "The books, and your capacity for understanding them, are just the same in all places."

29. On Resourcefulness

*Determine that the thing can and shall be done, and then
we shall find the way.*

Lincoln's resourcefulness probably sprang from his frontier
upbringing. When he was young, nothing came ready-made. If
you needed clothes, you made them. If you wanted to eat, you
found wild fruit, hunted game, or cultivated crops. If you
needed a boat, you built it. On the frontier, nature's response to
weak or hapless settlers was harsh, and human skeletons lit-
tered the old trails.

Lincoln was always resourceful. At the age of twenty-two,
he and two relatives made an agreement with a local entrepreneur to take a boat full of cargo down the Sangamon River to
the Mississippi and on to New Orleans. After building the
boat, they loaded it with pork in barrels, corn and hogs, and
embarked on their adventure. Unfortunately, not long after
launching, the boat snagged on a milldam.

All seemed lost. The boat was ready to sink. Then Lincoln suggested a plan. Unload the boat, except for the barrels,
he advised. Roll the barrels forward, then bore a small hole in
the end projecting over the dam. This, he theorized, would
allow the water to drain out of the boat. Sure enough, the boat
slid over the dam easily, they plugged the hole, and were soon
on their way—but not before an ecstatic entrepreneur had
announced to the gathered crowd that he would build a steam-

boat and Lincoln would be her captain. As a result of this experience, the young man would carry a can-do attitude with him for the rest of his life. "Lincoln thought that he could do anything that other men could or would try to do," Herndon observed. "He had unbounded confidence in himself, in his capacities and powers."

This resourceful stance would become apparent for the remainder of Lincoln's life. For example, in a speech before the U.S. House of Representatives in support of appropriations for bridges, roads, and canals, Lincoln quoted Terence, the Roman dramatist: "Attempt the end, and never stand to doubt. Nothing so hard, but search will find it out."

The first national paper currency—"greenbacks"—was issued at Lincoln's insistence, instituted as the last defense against financial collapse caused by the brutally expensive Civil War. When Secretary of the Treasury Salmon P. Chase objected on the grounds that the policy was unconstitutional, Lincoln replied, "These rebels are violating the Constitution to destroy the Union; I will violate the Constitution, if necessary, to save the Union." Chase admitted that he knew of no other way to raise the needed funds, and shortly afterward, the paper currency was issued.

30. On Ethics

It is [man's] duty to improve not only his own condition, but to assist in ameliorating mankind. . . . I am for those means which will give the greatest good to the greatest number.

A journalist named Noah Brooks, who came to know Lincoln in Washington, wrote: "With him the question was not, 'Is it convenient? Is it expedient?' but 'Is it right?'". Herndon's observations were similar: "What was true, good, and right, and just, he would never surrender; he would die before he would surrender his ideas of these."

Lincoln's strong ethical sensibility would dictate his behavior throughout his life. For example, during his Springfield years, a man by the name of King, who had just been elected a justice of the peace, came to see Lincoln for advice. What guiding principles should he follow, King wanted to know. Lincoln replied: "When you have a case between neighbors before you, listen well to all the evidence, stripping yourself of all prejudice, if any you have . . . hear the lawyers make their arguments as patiently as you can, and after the evidence and the lawyer's arguments are through, then stop one moment and ask yourself: What is justice in this case? and let your sense of justice be your decision. Law is nothing else but the best reason of wise men applied for ages to the transactions and business of mankind."

Having ethics, as Lincoln saw it, is to be in the right. Herndon has left us a quaint description of the way Lincoln applied this test to the practice of law: "When a client came into our office and wanted advice, Mr. Lincoln listened to his story well . . . now and then breaking in by asking a question. After the man was done telling his story fully and after Lincoln was done asking questions, he would generally think awhile before answering. When he answered, sometimes after he had taken time to do research, it was 'You are in the right,' or 'You are in the wrong.'"

31 . On Altruism

I have an irrepressible desire to live till I can be assured that the world is a little better for my having lived in it.

One of Lincoln's life goals was to do good and to be recognized for it. In one of his earliest campaign statements, he commented: "Every man is said to have his peculiar ambition. Whether it be true or not, I can say for one that I have no other so great as that of being truly esteemed of my fellow men, by rendering myself worthy of their esteem." Commentary by his contemporaries prove that he achieved this goal. Assistant Secretary of War Charles Dana stated: "The great quality of his appearance was benevolence and benignity: the wish to do somebody some good if he could."

Lincoln's vocation provided him with valuable tools to help people. As a lawyer, he could repair broken relationships, restore harmony where discord prevailed, and protect the weak and vulnerable. "As a peace-maker," he wrote, "the lawyer has a superior opportunity of being a good man."

For many people, a vocation is a way to make a living. For Lincoln, his vocation became a way to make a difference.

32. On Compassion

On the whole, my impression is that mercy bears richer fruits than any other attribute.

Lincoln was a strong President, and a gentle man. His best friend Joshua Speed observed that "Lincoln had the tenderest heart for any one in distress, whether man, beast, or bird."

Lincoln's friends liked to tell a story from his days on the judicial circuit to illustrate just how tenderhearted he was. One day while they were riding to the next courthouse, one of his associates noticed that their lanky companion had disappeared. "Where is Lincoln?" Back came the reply, "When I saw him last he had caught two young birds which the wind had blown out of their nest, and he has been hunting for the nest so as to put them back." Eventually, Lincoln rejoined the group. They began to tease him, but he replied, "I could not have slept well tonight if I had not saved those birds." Another time, he went back to pull a stranded pig out of the mire. Lincoln said he did it just to take a "pain" out of his mind.

Lincoln realized the irony of his situation. He who had returned baby birds to their nests was presiding over the bloodiest war imaginable. By war's end, more than a half-million men from the North and the South would lie dead. Tragically, he knew that he could have stopped the bloodshed any day with one stroke of his pen. As a result, he resolved to be as compassionate as he could be. Judge Ebenezer Peck recalled one visit to the White House when Lincoln seemed unusually upset. When asked why, Lincoln answered, "This is Friday. This day they execute farmers' boys for falling asleep at their posts. . . . If I say anything, they say I interfere with army discipline. Oh, I can't bear it, I can't bear it."

The word *compassion* is derived from two Latin words that mean "to suffer with." Lincoln epitomized the true meaning of that word.

33. On Trust

I expect the people to sustain me. They have never yet forsaken any true man.

Lincoln believed in "the people." He realized that the masses can be swayed by clever manipulators. But, like Jefferson, he also believed that in the long term, common people can rule themselves because they will use common sense. "The people will understand it," Lincoln often said. "Why should there not be a patient confidence in the ultimate justice of the people? Is there any better or equal hope in the world?" According to Joseph Gillespie, "Lincoln never idolized particular men but had wonderful faith in the honesty and good sense of the masses."

As President, he opened the White House to the people. He trusted people, liked people, and they trusted and liked him in return. They would stand in line for hours to petition for a job, complain, ask for favors, or just to shake his hand. He would greet a mechanic or clerk just as graciously as he would a governor. When a military officer suggested that all this was a waste of his time, Lincoln replied, "No hours of my day are better employed. . . . Men moving only in an official circle are apt to become merely official . . . [and] forget that they only hold power in a representative capacity. Now this is all wrong. I go into these promiscuous receptions of all who claim to have business with me twice each week, and every applicant for audience has to take his turn as if waiting to be shaved in a barber shop. . . . I call these receptions my 'public opinion baths.' . . ."

Lincoln believed in ordinary people, and never distanced himself from them. He was, after all, one of them, embodying all that they were and all that they could become. To deny their potential was to deny his. To believe in them was to believe in himself.

34. On Achievement

The way for a young man to rise is to improve himself every way he can, never suspecting that anybody wishes to hinder him.

Harriet Beecher Stowe called Lincoln's presidency "the greatest sign and marvel of our day." Here was a plain working man of the people who nevertheless "was conducting the passage of a great people through a crisis involving the destinies of the whole world."

Lincoln believed that the American ideal of the self-made man unleashed powerful economic forces and made achievement possible. "The prudent, penniless beginner in the world labors for wages awhile, saves a surplus with which to buy tools or land, for himself, then labors on his own account for another while, and at length hires another new beginner to help him. This . . . is *free* labor—the just and generous and prosperous system which opens the way for all—gives hope to all, and energy, and progress, and improvement of condition to all."

Lincoln was impressed by individuals who, like himself, were self-made. Frederick Douglass, the former slave who became internationally celebrated as an editor and orator, stated: "I account partially for his kindness to me because of the similarity with which I had fought my way up, we both starting at the lowest round of the ladder."

Lincoln felt that his own achievements should be an incentive for ordinary people everywhere. High achievement was not just for the privileged few. When a regiment of Ohio soldiers passed through Washington, Lincoln made this telling remark: "I happen temporarily to occupy this big White House. I am a living witness that any one of your children may look to come here as my father's child has."

35. On Citizenship

Let every American . . . swear by the blood of the Revolution
never to violate in the least particular the laws of the
country and never to tolerate their violation
by others.

The American experiment was about sixty years old when Lincoln delivered a remarkable speech in Springfield in 1838. Mob rule was very much on his mind. Riots and lynchings were occurring with increasing frequency all over the nation. In nearby Alton, Illinois, a mob had recently killed Elijah P. Lovejoy, the editor of an abolitionist paper.

The very existence of the nation was at stake, Lincoln believed, if individuals disobeyed laws with impunity or simply ignored them altogether. To do so, he reasoned, is to encourage anarchy or dictatorship. Like John Adams, Lincoln believed in "a government of laws and not of men." Though he realized that passion had once been critical in revolutionary times, he was convinced that "reason, cold, calculating, unimpassioned reason, must furnish all the materials for our future support and defence."

Lincoln urged "a reverence for the constitution and laws" in order to preserve what George Washington had begun. "Let reverence for the laws be breathed by every American mother to the lisping babe that prattles on her lap. . . . Let it become the *political religion* of the nation," he urged in his Springfield speech. Even bad laws, he said, "for the sake of example, should be religiously observed" until they can be repealed or changed. Lincoln never abandoned his reverence for the law or his belief that obeying the law is the duty of every citizen.

36. On Democracy

Government of the people, by the people, for the people. . . .

In Lincoln's mind, government is not something separate from the people. It is not something to be feared, ridiculed, or despised. Government is not *they*. It is *we the people*, so powerfully asserted in the Constitution. He himself memorably expressed this sentiment at Gettysburg.

The nation was still young when Lincoln was born. Most nations were still ruled by hereditary monarchs and aristocracies who looked upon the United States as a rash experiment. They believed democracy was inherently weak and confidently predicted that the young republic would soon collapse, just as the French Revolution had ended with a reign of terror. The Civil War seemed to prove that they were right.

Lincoln agreed that America was an experiment—a great, bold experiment. But he had faith that the experiment would prove once and for all that the people can govern themselves. "We proposed to give *all* a chance," Lincoln stated, "and we expected the weak to grow stronger, the ignorant, wiser; and all better and happier together. We made the experiment; and the fruit is before us."

Throughout history, it has been widely believed that ordinary people are fit only to be ruled, not rule. In America a democratic experiment was begun that demonstrated "the capability of a people to govern themselves," and offered individuals of every background a chance to take part in government. Thanks in large measure to Lincoln, the experiment continues, and enhances all our lives.

37. On Patriotism

*While pretending no indifference to earthly honors, I do claim
to be actuated in this contest by something higher than an
anxiety for office.*

Lincoln sought his country's good as well as his own. He was
proud to be a part of a revolutionary tradition that had brought
something new into the world—a tradition that promised all an
equal chance. As a young man, though, Lincoln had often felt
despondent about having done so little to perpetuate that tradition. "How hard, oh, how hard it is to die and leave one's
Country no better than if one had never lived for it," he told
Herndon. Though he had been a volunteer in the Black Hawk
War, and had served four terms in the Illinois State Legislature
plus one term in the U.S. House of Representatives, he felt
that this service paled in comparison to the sacrifices of Revolutionary War heroes.

On his way from Springfield to be inaugurated President,
Lincoln told a gathering in Trenton, New Jersey, about the
account of the Revolutionary War that he read as a boy in
Weems's *Life of Washington*. Lincoln stated: "I shall be most
happy indeed if I shall be an humble instrument in the hands of
the Almighty, and of this, his almost chosen people, for perpet-
uating the object of that great struggle," he told the crowd. The
next day in Philadelphia, Lincoln made the chilling assertion

that he would rather be assassinated than to surrender the great principles embodied in the Declaration of Independence.

Joseph Gillespie recalled that Lincoln loved "our government and its founders almost to idolatry." Love of country ennobled Lincoln. That patriotic principle—that larger moral purpose—transformed him from a sometimes unexceptional politician into a statesman.

38. On Tolerance

This good earth is plenty broad enough for white man and negro both, and there is no need of either pushing the other off.

When Lincoln was young, the American frontier was still a vast, sparsely populated region. The residents of the little frontier settlements generally welcomed people who possessed needed skills—despite their diversity. One person could shoe a horse and another could make a shoe, one person could grow potatoes and another could sell them. One could teach and another could learn. The early inhabitants tolerated one another because they needed one another. If they were to exist, they had to coexist.

Lincoln never lost that frontier attitude, which may have been reinforced by the Bible passage: "Thou shalt not oppress a stranger: for ye know the heart of a stranger, seeing ye were strangers in the land of Egypt." As far as he was concerned, being a stranger was not sufficient justification to exclude or hate someone. His acceptance of people unlike him in color, creed, or language was indeed impressive. The abolitionist orator and former slave Frederick Douglass observed that "[Lincoln] was the first great man that I have talked with in the United States who in no single instance reminded me of the difference between himself and myself, of the difference of color."

Lincoln's open-mindedness was apparent even before he became President. For example, when an anti-immigrant and anti-Catholic political organization called Know Nothings became popular, Lincoln was asked how he felt about the movement. He responded, "Our progress in degeneracy appears to me to be pretty rapid. As a nation, we began by declaring that '*all men are created equal.*' We now practically read it 'all men are created equal, *except negroes.*' When the Know Nothings get control, it will read 'all men are created equal, except negroes, *and foreigners, and catholics.*'" Three days after signing the Emancipation Proclamation on January 1, 1863, Lincoln rescinded General Grant's notorious order that banned Jewish merchants "as a class" from military camps in Tennessee.

Though Lincoln understood that members of a diverse population will have problems adjusting to one another, he was also wise enough to see that diversity provides an enormous opportunity to utilize the strengths of many individuals and cultures.

39. On Idealism

Something in that Declaration [gave] liberty, not alone to the people of this country, but hope to all the world, and for all future time.

If ever there was an idealist, it was Lincoln. He lived under the spell of great values. He believed in God and endeavored to do what he perceived was His will. He believed in his country and in the great principles articulated in the Declaration of Independence. He believed that ordinary people could both improve and rule themselves.

Lincoln admired what the nation's founders had done to ensure that the mistakes of the Old World would not be repeated in the New, and felt sure that their dream was achievable. In order to make a fresh beginning, the founders had chosen to protect human rights through written assurances and guarantees. Yet as idealistic as many of them were, their vision had not been fully realized. Slavery, with all its horrors, still existed. Lincoln lived long enough to see it end. At his urging, Congress passed the Thirteenth Amendment, which guaranteed the end of slavery in America. Thus he contributed to the list of human rights that the Constitution affirms and protects.

Lincoln's idealism was tempered by a deep understanding of human nature. In the courtroom and in politics, he was constantly exposed to the seamy side of life. Nevertheless, "There was no flabby philanthropy about Abraham Lincoln," wrote

Charles Dana. Additionally, Lincoln's idealism helped him rise above anger and vindictiveness. "I shall do nothing in malice," he said. "What I deal with is too great for malicious dealing." Dana would later comment that "he was all solid, hard, keen intelligence combined with goodness."

Idealism would also help Lincoln to persevere in spite of numerous setbacks and losses. After his death, David Davis, who by then had become a U.S. Supreme Court justice, wrote this assessment of his old friend: "Believing in certain great principles of government, he did not complain because they were unacceptable to the people, having faith in their ultimate triumph."

40. On Self-Reliance

*Forget that you have anyone to fall back upon, and
you will do justice to yourself and your client.*

Lincoln knew that self-reliance and authority go hand in hand.
A great leader is assertive, and he was confident in his calm
decisiveness. Ironically enough, the strong individuals Lincoln
selected for his cabinet at first thought he was too weak for the
job. Mary Lincoln told her husband that friends of his secretary of state, William H. Seward, were boasting that Seward
would rule Lincoln. The President replied: "I may not rule,
myself, but certainly Seward shall not. The only ruler I have is
my conscience—following God in it—and these men will have
to learn that yet."

Lincoln was made of stern stuff and could assert himself
vigorously when he needed to. For example, when the residence
of Postmaster General Montgomery Blair was burned by a
Confederate raid, Blair harshly criticized Union officers.
Blair's enemies demanded that Lincoln dismiss Blair for his
comments. Lincoln responded: "I must myself be the judge
how long to retain in and when to remove any of you from his
position. It would greatly pain me to discover any of you
endeavoring to procure another's removal, or in any way to
prejudice him before the public. Such endeavor would be a
wrong to me; and, much worse, a wrong to the country. My

wish is that on this subject no remark be made, nor question asked, by any of you, here or elsewhere, now or hereafter."

Assistant Secretary of War Charles Dana, who observed Lincoln with his cabinet, generals, and other officials wrote: "To every one he was pleasant and cordial. Yet they all felt it was his word that went at last; that every case was open until he gave his decision. This impression of authority, of reserve force, Mr. Lincoln always gave to those about him." David Davis concurred: "He was a self-possessed man," he wrote. "He thought for himself."

41. On Piety

I have had so many evidences of [H]is direction, so many instances when I have been controlled by some other power than my own will, that I cannot doubt that this power comes from above.

No issue in Lincoln's life has raised more questions than his religious belief, or lack thereof. Political opponents often seized on his failure to join any particular church as evidence of atheism. Rumors circulated that as a young man Lincoln had written a scandalous manuscript denying the truth of the Bible. (He later drafted a statement stating that he was not an enemy of religion.) Some of his close friends maintained that Lincoln remained a skeptic, or a deist, till the day he died. Others claimed that he had a conversion experience. The debate still continues, even today.

Although Lincoln was not a religious man in the most traditional sense of the word, he was deeply spiritual. His wife Mary said he was "a religious man by nature," and referred to his personal faith as "a kind of poetry." Both publicly and privately, he expressed deep reliance on God. He attended church frequently, read the Bible, memorized many of its passages, and prayed regularly.

During his years in Springfield, Lincoln was called to the bedside of a dying woman to draw up her will. When he had finished the document, she asked if he would read to her from the Bible. Someone offered him a Bible, but he waved it away, and recited the Twenty-third Psalm from memory.

In the White House, particularly after the death of his son Willie, Lincoln's reliance upon God deepened. References to Almighty God became a regular part of his conversations and writings. Found among his papers was this meditation on the divine will, written in early 1862: "The will of God prevails. . . . In the present civil war it is quite possible that God's purpose is something different from the purpose of either party. . . . I am almost ready to say this is probably true—that God wills this contest, and wills that it shall not end yet." Lincoln eventually made public these thoughts from his private musings in the eloquent words of the Second Inaugural Address. (See p. 123.)

Although Lincoln acknowledged God's purpose in human affairs, his response was far from one of passive acquiescence. "It has pleased Almighty God to place me in my present position," he told Noyes W. Miner, a Springfield minister and neighbor of the Lincoln's for several years. "Looking up to Him for wisdom and divine guidance, I must work out my destiny as best I can."

4 2. On Timing

I shall go just so fast and only so fast as I think I'm right and the people are ready for the step.

As a boy, Lincoln had read and internalized the Shakespearian observation that "there is a tide in the affairs of men, which, taken at the flood, leads on to fortune. We must take the current when it serves, or lose our ventures." And like all successful leaders, he grasped the importance of timing. His very election as President relied on it; had he run four years earlier, the newly formed Republican Party would have been too weak and he too unknown to win the race. Additionally, he observed as a state legislator and as a congressman that timing is essential in order to get bills passed. "Time was Lincoln's Prime Minister," wrote Schuyler Colfax, Speaker of the House. "He always waited, as a wise man should wait, until the right moment brought up his reserves."

But nothing illustrates Lincoln's mastery of this concept better than his strategy for emancipation. Some of his advisers thought that he should make such a proclamation immediately after becoming President. Others disagreed, saying that he lacked the constitutional authority to do so. Even if he did, they argued, emancipation would leave hundreds of thousands of displaced slaves unemployed and destitute, and might ignite a bloody race war. Thousands of troops had volunteered, not to abolish slavery, but to save the Union. Many of Lincoln's advisers feared they might lay down their arms if the contest were defined as a crusade to end slavery. Lincoln listened to all the arguments and concluded that the time had not come for such a move. Not yet. As a master strategist, he realized that many ideas fail, not because they are bad ideas, but because they are broached at the wrong time.

There were other factors in Lincoln's decision. He reasoned that European nations, which were closely watching events in America, might conclude that the Emancipation Proclamation was a desperate act by a government that had lost control. With Union forces suffering one defeat after another, that analysis would have been understandable. Lincoln realized he should wait for a victory, and when Union forces had finally repulsed the Confederate army at Antietam, Lincoln decided that the time had come.

When the proclamation finally went into effect, morale remained high and, in fact, increased dramatically. Lincoln later said: "It is my conviction that, had the [emancipation] proclamation been issued even six months earlier than it was, public sentiment would not have sustained it."

43. On Adversity

I find quite as much material for a lecture in those points wherein I have failed, as in those wherein I have been moderately successful.

Over the course of his life, Lincoln realized that failure is essential to learning. Fascinated by science, he knew that scientific knowledge progresses by trial and error—through more experiments that fail than succeed. One day in Springfield, Lincoln observed his partner reading *The Annual of Science* and asked to look at the book. After a few minutes Lincoln commented that it seemed better than many because it reported failed experiments: "Too often we read only of successful experiments in science and philosophy, whereas if the history of failure and defeat was included there would be a saving of brain work as well as time."

Lincoln often applied that concept to his own life. Often critical of Lincoln, Horace Greeley admitted that "he was open to all impressions and influences, and gladly profited by the teachings of events and circumstances, no matter how adverse or unwelcome. There was probably no year of his life when he was not a wiser, cooler, and better man than he had been the year preceding."

Lincoln also saw failure as an installment on later success. He was defeated in 1832, the first time he ran for the Illinois legislature, but he came back to win in 1834, and was reelected in 1836, 1838, and 1840. Years later, in a campaign that attracted national attention, he lost his bid for the U.S. Senate to Stephen Douglas, but came back in 1860 to defeat Douglas for the presidency.

Just because Lincoln learned to view failures pragmatically doesn't mean they were pleasant. Often they hurt him deeply. Stephen Logan, one of Lincoln's law partners, recalled a courtroom defeat Lincoln suffered at the hands of Edward D. Baker. "He came and complained to me that Baker had got so much the start of him that he despaired of getting even with him in acquirements and skill. I said to him: 'It does not depend on the start a man gets, it depends on how he keeps up his labors and efforts until middle life'. . . . Baker was a brilliant man but very negligent; while Lincoln was growing all the time."

Failures sometimes occur in situations that provide little chance of winning. Nevertheless, Lincoln believed that one must struggle, simply because it is the right thing to do. Though Lincoln did in fact experience many failures, as all restlessly ambitious individuals do, far more important is the way in which he faced them.

44. On Deliberation

I am never easy now, when I am handling a thought, till I have bounded it north and bounded it south, and bounded it east and bounded it west.

Lincoln was neither quick nor impulsive. By his own admission, he was slow to learn, but he was also slow to forget what he had learned. One day in the White House, he and his wife's cousin Elizabeth Todd Grimsley watched while his son Willie quietly pondered a problem and then beamed when he had solved it. "I know every step of the process by which that boy arrived at his satisfactory solution," Lincoln commented. "It is by just such slow methods I attain results."

Horace Greeley said that Lincoln possessed "one of those minds that work, not quickly nor brilliantly, but exhaustively." Many lawyers who worked with him agreed that he was neither intuitive nor brilliant, but instead systematic, painstaking, and careful. "His habit was, before speaking or acting, to deliberately look through, around and beyond every object, fact, statement, or proposition to which his attention was called," Herndon observed.

Deliberation brought some important benefits, Lincoln discovered. He made fewer mistakes by not rushing. "I am a slow walker," he said, "but I never walk back." In response to a letter urging him to "stand firm," Lincoln responded: "I hope to 'stand firm' enough not to go backward, and yet not go forward fast enough to wreck the country's cause." This approach would carry over into his decision-making. "He would listen to everybody; he would hear everybody; but he rarely, if ever, asked for opinions," Leonard Swett recalled. "As a politician and as President, he arrived at all his conclusions from his own reflections, and when his opinion was once formed, he never doubted that it was right."

45. On Research

When I have a particular case in hand, I . . . love to dig up the question by the roots and hold it up and dry it before the fires of the mind.

Nat Grigsby, one of Lincoln's boyhood friends, remembered that Lincoln "thoroughly read his books whilst we played." Whenever Lincoln joined his companions, they would cluster around him to hear him talk. Perhaps those childhood experiences taught Lincoln that having superior information gives one an advantage over his peers.

This lesson would be reinforced early on when he worked as the junior partner of Stephen T. Logan, one of the greatest lawyers of his day. Logan urged Lincoln not to rely on his wits alone, but to prepare each case carefully, anticipating his opponent's arguments. He urged Lincoln to study a case from the viewpoint of his opponent. Lincoln accepted the lesson and later said that he was never again surprised by an adversary's contentions. This habit stood him well in his famous debates with U.S. Senator Stephen Douglas, who at the time had become known as the most formidable orator in the nation. Lincoln had so mastered Douglas's arguments that he often turned them to his own advantage.

What Logan urged him to do in the courtroom became a lifelong habit. According to Robert Rantoul, Lincoln wanted to know "every seam and joint in the armor of any public man with whom he might possibly be called upon to break a lance."

46. On Conviction

The world shall know that I will keep my faith to friends and enemies, come what will.

Alexander H. Stephens, who became Vice President of the Confederacy, described Lincoln as "a man of strong convictions, and what Carlyle would have called an earnest man." That earnestness became evident in the turbulent years just before the outbreak of the Civil War. During this period, when Lincoln became deeply committed to the cause of halting slavery's spread into the new territories of the nation, he was transformed from a regional politician into a national force. The slavery issue reached his heart, and from then onward, Lincoln's message possessed new urgency and power.

His listeners could feel Lincoln's commitment. A young man, Henry McPike, observed the last public debate between Douglas and Lincoln at Alton, Illinois. McPike, who later became mayor of Alton, remembered Lincoln's speech: "It seemed to me there came an eloquence born of the earnestness of a heart convinced of the sinfulness—the injustice and the brutality of the institution of slavery, which made him a changed man. So long as I live I will never lose the impression he made upon me." Lincoln had discovered what all great communicators know—that before they can move others, they must themselves be moved.

47. On Freedom

I intend no modification of my oft-expressed personal wish
that all men everywhere could be free.

Like Jefferson, Lincoln loved freedom and detested all forms of
tyranny. As a young man, he enthusiastically embraced many of
the powerful revolutionary ideas that were sweeping through
the Western world, and would argue for hours about their
implications in New Salem's debating society. Many of his atti-
tudes were shaped by Thomas Paine, who wrote in *The Age of
Reason*, "I believe in the equality of man; and I believe that religious duties consist in doing justice, loving mercy, and endeavoring to make our fellow-creatures happy."

For Lincoln, the concept of the equality of man and the
concept of freedom were inextricably linked. If all are born
equal, he reasoned, then no individual has the right to dominate
another just because he is born to a higher station in life. Slavery, which was legal in some states and spreading to the territories, was a flagrant contradiction of that fundamental idea.
Americans had become "hypocrites" before the world, Lincoln
stated in one of his speeches, "by fostering human slavery and
proclaiming ourselves, at the same time, the sole friends of
human freedom." He developed that idea in a letter: "Those
who deny freedom to others deserve it not for themselves; and,
under a just God, can not long retain it."

Freedom is right and tyranny is wrong, Lincoln believed,

among governments, churches, slaveholders, or even parents. He was convinced that it was the destiny of the United States to demonstrate that truth, and told Congress, "We shall nobly save, or meanly lose, the last best, hope of earth." And the benefits of emancipation should not just be limited to the slaves; it should be used to create a safe climate where other free institutions could thrive. "In *giving* freedom to the *slave*," Lincoln stated to Congress, "we *assure* freedom to the *free*—honorable alike in what we give, and what we preserve."

48. On Self-Discipline

Will springs from the two elements of moral sense and self-interest.

For Lincoln, willpower was shaped by the guiding force of self-discipline. And self-discipline created the needed balance in his life between freedom and responsibility. Though he resisted restraints imposed by others, he willingly imposed restraints upon himself, perhaps as a result of his childhood training. Inner direction was a dominant theme in nineteenth-century American life, inculcated in the schools by frequent repetition of proverbs and assigned reading of maxims, and in the churches by pastors and evangelists. In Murray's *English Reader*, Lincoln may well have come upon this maxim: "What avails the show of external liberty to one who has lost the government of himself?"

The need for self-discipline was powerfully emphasized by the environment. In the sparsely settled frontier, where external sources of control were few and weak, settlers internalized a sense of self-control, which was motivated by survival. No one needed to stand over those hardy pioneers to tell them they had to hunt and plant and be frugal if they wished to eat.

In Lincoln's quest to make the most of himself, he took on the arduous task of mastering English grammar and legal theory in order to become a respected lawyer. Later on, long after he had become a successful lawyer, he decided to study Euclid in order to be more precise and powerful in his logic. In New Salem, when he had virtually no possessions, he recognized that his capacity to make a resolution and keep it was perhaps his most valuable asset. For Lincoln, self-discipline was inextricably linked to willpower. In a letter written two years before his election to the presidency, remembering a lifetime of commitment, Lincoln advised: "By all means, don't say 'if I can'; say 'I *will*.'"

49. On Humor

Laughter [is] the joyous, beautiful, universal evergreen of life.

Lincoln had a famous laugh—rollicking, high-pitched, and loud. He loved funny stories, and when it came to telling one, few could surpass him. Lincoln often would tell one droll story after another, leaving his listeners convulsed with laughter. While still in Springfield, Lincoln stated, "It was a common notion that those who laughed heartily and often never amounted to much—never made great men." He paused, then added, "If this be the case, farewell to all my glory."

Lincoln was always fond of humor. His childhood acquaintances remembered that he would sometimes stand on a log or stump and mimic the preacher's sermons, much to their delight. After he became a lawyer, he perfected his skill in great storytelling bouts at the taverns and hotels on the judicial circuit, where he was known as one of the best.

Lincoln sometimes chided his cabinet members for being too serious. "Gentlemen, why don't you laugh?" he asked when they responded glumly to his reading of a humorous piece by the writer Artemus Ward. He used humor to find a way into people's hearts, a way to connect with them. Like any good salesman, he understood that smiling people are more likely to make purchases or accept ideas than frowning ones.

Long before scientific evidence proved that laughter can actually prevent disease and sometimes cure it, Lincoln spoke of laughter as medicine. He realized that laughter could be an anesthetic that would help him bear pain. Congressman Isaac N. Arnold remembered hearing Lincoln's distinctive laughter ringing through the White House while he and a delegation waited to be admitted to the President's office. He remarked: "That laugh has been the President's life-preserver."

50. On Friendship

The better part of one's life consists of his friendships.

Lincoln knew how to make friends and keep them. He enjoyed companionship, and had an uncanny ability to attract people. His many friends offered to do all sorts of generous things for him—for example, loaning him money, giving him free lodging, recommending him for important offices, and helping him get elected to office.

People recognized that Lincoln had their best interests at heart. If he could not help them, they correctly sensed that he certainly would never deliberately hurt them. He could be trusted with a secret or with money, and he was neither greedy nor envious. He was a grateful man and showed his appreciation for any little kindness in memorable and appropriate ways. He took the time to write a personal letter to a young girl named Grace Bedell, thanking her for advising him to grow a beard. He also remembered a kindness shown him when he was a poor newcomer to New Salem by a local leader named Jack Armstrong. Years later, when Armstrong's son was indicted for murder, Lincoln became his defense lawyer. During the course of his successful defense, he told the jury with tear-filled eyes, how kind his client's father had been to him in his youth.

To these fundamental principles of care, loyalty, and generosity, Lincoln added his skill as a conversationalist, which also made him a sought-after friend. He knew how to listen, and when he listened, he listened attentively. But he also became an excellent talker, and could entertain individuals or groups by the hour, punctuating his narratives with energetically told quips and stories.

Although he was gregarious, Lincoln cherished solitude. His practice of regularly withdrawing from others' company, instead of isolating him, actually made his acquaintances want to be with him more. "Where is Lincoln?" was a frequently asked question on the judicial circuit and in Springfield. During those sometimes protracted quiet times, Lincoln would recharge himself, and eventually return to the company of his friends.

Friendships require time to sustain. Despite a back-breaking work schedule, Lincoln maintained an extensive correspondence with numerous acquaintances, in addition to spending long hours face-to-face with those he cared about most. He freely gave his advice and his time to a wide assortment of claimants.

51. On Charity

With charity for all . . .

The end of the Civil War was clearly in sight when Lincoln spoke these famous words in his second inaugural address. He realized that many northern leaders were clamoring for him to make the Confederate leaders pay dearly for the bloodshed they had caused. Even prominent clergymen were calling for vengeance. But instead of yielding to the pressure, Lincoln huddled with General Grant and General Sherman, stipulating that when victory came, they should extend the most liberal surrender terms imaginable. The men in gray would be allowed to return to their homes with their horses, mules, and their self-respect.

These simple words eloquently describe Lincoln's greatest virtue. Eights weeks later, they would be repeated at his funeral in Springfield, Illinois. In the nineteenth century, the word *charity* meant far more than philanthropy; it was understood to be the highest form of love that a human being can express. A charitable person was kind, patient, liberal in judging the behavior of others, never haughty nor greedy, always generous.

Lincoln had grown up on the words of the King James Version of the Bible, and knew this famous passage by heart: "Though I speak with the tongues of men and of angels, and have not charity, I am become as sounding brass and a tinkling cymbal. . . . And now abideth faith, hope, charity, these three; but the greatest of these is charity."

Lincoln's charity was the rule, not the exception. Charity is what one feels, but it is also what one does. Lincoln manifested this all-important virtue in little words and actions as well as big ones. It is part of his greatness—both as a man and as a leader.

52. On Life's Brevity

Time is everything.

With Lincoln, time consciousness was almost an obsession. Keenly aware of the brevity of life, he himself was constantly surrounded by death. He observed firsthand how quickly life could be snuffed out. When he was two years old, his infant brother died; he lost his mother when he was nine. When he was ten years old, he had a near-death experience: he was kicked by a horse and, in his own words, was "apparently killed for a time." He lost his sister Sarah when he was eighteen. Ann Rutledge—his friend and, according to Herndon, his first and best romantic love—died when he was twenty-six. In 1850, his son "Eddy" died at age three. During the course of the Civil War, scores of relatives and close friends were slain in battle. And in 1862, his beloved eleven-year-old son Willie died, a loss that devastated the President.

Lincoln often quoted a passage from Gibbon's "Philosophical Reflections," which contains the statement: "In a composition of some days . . . the duration of a life or reign is contracted to a fleeting moment. The grave is ever beside the throne." His favorite poem, "Mortality," by William Knox, dwells on the transient nature of life. Lincoln memorized the entire poem as a young man and recited it so often that many people believed that he was the author. In the words of the poem, human existence is a "swift-fleeing meteor, a fast-flying cloud." It was a metaphor that would have tragic significance in his own life.

"Billy, I feel as if I shall meet with some terrible end," he told his law partner before he left for Washington. When Harriet Beecher Stowe, author of *Uncle Tom's Cabin*, came to visit the President, they talked about the Civil War. Before the influential author departed, Lincoln remarked, "Whichever way it ends, I have the impression that I sha'n't last long after it's over."

His premonition would prove to be correct. But so would his desire to leave the world a little better. When he expired at twenty-two minutes past seven on Saturday morning, April 15, 1865, Abraham Lincoln left much to show for the time he had spent here: the slaves had been freed, the Union had been preserved, and the nation had been reborn.

Afterword

If the end brings me out all right, what is said against me won't amount to anything. If the end brings me out wrong, ten angels swearing I was right would make no difference.

Careers, like symphonies and books, cannot be fully evaluated until they are finished. The more unconventional a symphony, a book, or a life, the less obvious its ending.

Lincoln's life was always a work in progress. Had he died even a year earlier, historians today would probably call him a well-meaning but tragic figure. Without a last-minute success on the battlefield, Lincoln would have been defeated at the polls. He had even written out plans for the transition. His successor would probably have ended the war by recognizing the Confederacy, thereby dismantling the Union and leaving slavery in place. But a major last-minute victory did come at Atlanta, and Lincoln sealed his place in history.

When Thomas Jefferson died in 1826, he lamented the loss of his associates who had invented the United States. "All, all dead," Jefferson despaired on his deathbed, "and ourselves left alone amidst a new generation whom we know not and who knows not us." He could not have known that, at that very moment, a young rustic on the Indiana frontier was getting to know him. Who indeed could have predicted that the barely literate youth would grow up and engrave Jefferson's words on the hearts of the world at Gettysburg?

Nor could Jefferson have known that the great American experiment would survive, or that this boy, inspired by his words, would play such a central part in preserving it. When Lincoln visited the Confederate capital of Richmond shortly after it fell, he stayed for only a few hours. It was clear that the Union had been preserved and slavery was no more. The nation was being reborn.

On his return to Washington aboard the steamboat *River Queen*, the President read poetry to some of his friends. One of the passages was from *Macbeth*, his favorite of all Shakespeare's plays. Little did he realize the eerie significance it would have for his own life.

Duncan is in his grave;
After life's fitful fever he sleeps well.
Treason has done his worst. Nor steel nor poison,
Malice domestic, foreign levy, nothing,
Can touch him further.

Six days later, Lincoln was struck down by an assassin's bullet. Like Duncan, nothing could touch him further. His voice was silenced. But still he speaks.

Excerpts from Selected Speeches and Writings of Lincoln

Lincoln's Soliloquy

When Lincoln was thirty-five, he traveled to his boyhood home in Indiana, where he made several political speeches. That visit aroused in him a profound feeling that he later expressed in these words:

> My childhood's home I see again,
> And sadden with the view;
> And still, as memory crowds my brain,
> There's pleasure in it too.
>
> O Memory! thou midway world
> 'Twixt earth and paradise,
> Where things decayed and loved ones lost
> In dreamy shadows rise,
>
> And, freed from all that's earthly vile,
> Seem hallowed, pure, and bright,
> Like scenes in some enchanted isle
> All bathed in liquid light.

As dusky mountains please the eye
When twilight chases day;
As bugle-notes that, passing by,
In distance die away;

As leaving some grand waterfall,
We, lingering, list its roar—
So memory will hallow all
We've known, but know no more.

Near twenty years have passed away
Since here I bid farewell
To woods and fields, and scenes of play,
And playmates loved so well.

Where many were, but few remain
Of old familiar things;
But seeing them, to mind again
The lost and absent brings.

The friends I left that parting day,
How changed, as time has sped!
Young childhood grown, strong manhood gray,
And half of all are dead.

I hear the loved survivors tell
How nought from death could save,
Till every sound appears a knell,
And every spot a grave.

I range the fields with pensive tread,
And pace the hollow rooms
And feel (companion of the dead)
I'm living in the tombs.

The "House Divided" Speech

Delivered on June 16, 1858, during his campaign for the U.S. Senate against Stephen Douglas, the following words from the introduction of his speech proved to be prophetic. They seemed incendiary at the time and may have caused Lincoln's defeat.

If we could first know *where* we are, and *whither* we are tending, we could then better judge *what* to do, and *how* to do it. . . . "A house divided against itself cannot stand." I believe this government cannot endure, permanently half *slave* and half *free*. I do not expect the Union to be *dissolved*—I do not expect the house to *fall*—but I *do* expect it will cease to be divided. It will become *all* one thing, or *all* the other. . . .

The Farewell Address in Springfield

Spoken on February 11, 1861, at the Springfield railway station as Lincoln was about to depart on the greatest challenge of his career, the presidency of the United States.

My friends—No one, not in my situation, can appreciate my feeling of sadness at this parting. To this place, and the kindness of these people, I owe every thing. Here I have lived a quarter of a century, and have passed from a young to an old man. Here my children have been born, and one is buried. I now leave, not knowing when, or whether ever, I may return, with a task before me greater than that which rested upon Washington. Without the assistance of that Divine Being who ever attended him, I cannot succeed. With that assistance I cannot fail. Trusting in Him, who can go with me, and remain with you and be every where for good, let us confidently hope that all will yet be well. To His care commending you, as I hope in your prayers you will commend me, I bid you an affectionate farewell.

The First Inaugural Address

Delivered on March 4, 1861, under the approaching storm cloud of civil war: seven Southern states had already seceded from the Union, and South Carolina had demanded that Federal troops abandon Fort Sumter.

. . . My countrymen, one and all, think calmly and *well,* upon this whole subject. Nothing valuable can be lost by taking time. . . . In *your* hands, my dissatisfied fellow countrymen, and not in *mine,* is the momentous issue of civil war. The government will not assail *you*. You can have no conflict, without being yourselves the aggressors. *You* have no oath registered in Heaven to destroy the government, while I shall have the most solemn one to "preserve, protect and defend" it.

I am loathe to close. We are not enemies, but friends. We must not be enemies. Though passion may have strained, it must not break our bonds of affection. The mystic chords of memory, stretching from every battle-field, and patriot grave, to every living heart and hearthstone, all over this broad land, will yet swell the chorus of the Union, when again touched, as surely they will be, by the better angels of our nature.

The Annual Message to Congress, 1862

Presented on December 1, 1862, this message contained a number of proposals, including one to compensate any state that emancipated its slaves. The following excerpt is the message's memorable conclusion.

. . . Fellow-citizens, *we* cannot escape history. We of this Congress and this administration, will be remembered in spite of ourselves. No personal significance, or insignificance, can spare one or another of us. The fiery trial through which we pass, will light us down, in honor or dishonor, to the latest generation. We *say* we are for the Union. The world will not forget that we say this. We know how to save the Union. The world knows we do know how to save it. We—even *we here*—hold the power, and bear the responsibility. In *giving* freedom to the *slave,* we *assure* freedom to the *free*— honorable alike in what we give, and what we preserve. We shall nobly save, or meanly lose, the last best, hope of earth. Other means may succeed; this could not fail. The way is plain, peaceful, generous, just—a way which, if followed, the world will forever applaud, and God must forever bless.

The Final Emancipation Proclamation

On September 22, 1862, Lincoln read to a startled cabinet a preliminary version of the Emancipation Proclamation, which stated that slaves in all portions of the nation still in rebellion on January 1, 1863, would be freed. It was publicly announced the following day, and, as promised, went into effect on the first day of 1863.

A Proclamation

". . . On the first day of January, in the year of our Lord one thousand eight hundred and sixty-three, all persons held as slaves within any State, or designated part of a State, the people whereof shall then be in rebellion against the United States, shall be then, thenceforward, and forever free; and the Executive Government of the United States, including the military and naval authority thereof, will recognize and maintain the freedom of such persons, and will do no act or acts to repress such persons, or any of them, in any efforts they may make for their actual freedom. . . ."

Now, therefore, I, Abraham Lincoln, President of the United States, by virtue of the power in me vested as Commander-in-Chief, of the Army and Navy of the United States in time of actual armed rebellion against authority and government of the United States, and as a fit and necessary war measure for suppressing said rebellion, do . . . order and declare that all persons held as slaves within said designated States, and parts of States, are, and henceforward shall be free; and that the Executive government of the United States, including the military and naval authorities thereof, will recognize and maintain the freedom of said persons.

And I hereby enjoin upon the people so declared to be free to abstain from all violence, unless in necessary self-defense; and I recommend to them that, in all cases when allowed, they labor faithfully for reasonable wages.

And I further declare and make known, that such persons of suitable condition, will be received into the armed service of the United States to garrison forts, positions, stations, and other places, and to man vessels of all sorts in said service. . . .

The Gettysburg Address

*The historic battle of Gettysburg was fought on July 1–3, 1863.
When the military cemetery was dedicated on November 19,
1863, the noted orator Edward Everett was asked to deliver the
principal address. The President was asked to give a "few appropriate remarks."*

Four score and seven years ago our fathers brought
forth on this continent, a new nation, conceived in
Liberty, and dedicated to the proposition that all
men are created equal.

Now we are engaged in a great civil war, testing
whether that nation, or any nation so conceived and
so dedicated, can long endure. We are met on a
great battle-field of that war. We have come to dedicate a portion of that field, as a final resting place
for those who here gave their lives that that nation
might live. It is altogether fitting and proper that we
should do this.

But, in a larger sense we can not dedicate—we
can not consecrate—we can not hallow—this
ground. The brave men, living and dead, who strug-
gled here, have consecrated it, far above our poor
power to add or detract. The world will little note,
nor long remember what we say here, but it can
never forget what they did here. It is for us the living,
rather, to be dedicated here to the unfinished work
which they who fought here have thus far so nobly
advanced. It is rather for us to be here dedicated to

the great task remaining before us—that from these honored dead we take increased devotion to that cause for which they here gave the last full measure of devotion—that we here highly resolve that these dead shall not have died in vain—that this nation, under God, shall have a new birth of freedom—and that government of the people, by the people, for the people, shall not perish from the earth.

The Second Inaugural Address

This speech was delivered on March 4, 1865, after a series of major successes by Union forces, when the war's end was in sight. Considered by many to be one of the most eloquent statements ever written in the English language, the words were repeated eight weeks later in Springfield, Illinois, at Lincoln's funeral.

. . . On the occasion corresponding to this four years ago, all thoughts were anxiously directed to an impending civil-war. All dreaded it—all sought to avert it. . . . Both parties deprecated war; but one of them would *make* war rather than let the nation survive; and the other would *accept* war rather than let it perish. And the war came.

. . . Neither party expected for the war, the magnitude, or the duration, which it has already attained. . . . Each looked for an easier triumph, and a result less fundamental and astounding.

Both read the same Bible, and pray to the same God; and each invokes His aid against the other. It may seem strange that any men should dare to ask a just God's assistance in wringing their bread from the sweat of other men's faces; but let us judge not that we be not judged. The prayers of both could not be answered; that of neither has been answered fully. The Almighty has His own purposes. "Woe unto the world because of offences! for it must needs be that offences come; but woe to that man by whom the offence cometh!" If we shall suppose that American Slavery is one of those offences which, in the providence of God, must needs come, but which, having continued through His appointed time, He now wills to remove, and that He gives to both North and South, this terrible war, as the woe due to those by whom the offence came, shall we discern therein any departure from those divine attributes which the believers in a Living God always ascribe to Him? Fondly do we hope—fervently do we pray—that this mighty scourge of war may speedily pass away. Yet, if God wills that it continue, until all the wealth piled by the bond-man's two hundred and fifty years of unrequited toil shall be sunk, and until every drop of blood drawn with the lash, shall be paid by another drawn with the sword, as was said three thousand years ago, so still it must be said "the judgments of the Lord, are true and righteous altogether."

With malice toward none; with charity for all;

with firmness in the right, as God gives us to see the right, let us strive on to finish the work we are in; to bind up the nation's wounds; to care for him who shall have borne the battle, and for his widow, and his orphan—to do all which may achieve and cherish a just, and a lasting peace, among ourselves, and with all nations.

BIOGRAPHICAL NOTES

Abram Bergen
(1836–1906) Lawyer and judge who met Lincoln on the Eighth Judicial Circuit; subsequently moved to Topeka, Kansas, where he died.

Noah Brooks
(1830–1903) Washington correspondent for the *Sacramento Daily Union*; scheduled to become Lincoln's private secretary in his second term. Later published *Washington in Lincoln's Time* (1895), based on his newspaper dispatches.

Francis B. Carpenter
(1830–1900) Painted the *First Reading of the Emancipation Proclamation of President Lincoln* and later wrote *Six Months at the White House with Abraham Lincoln*, based in part on conversations he had with the President while painting him.

Schuyler Colfax
(1823–1884) Served seven consecutive terms in Congress, and was made Speaker in 1863; reelected in 1865 and 1867. He served as Vice President with President Grant.

Elizabeth Crawford
(1806–1892) Knew Lincoln as a boy; he worked for her husband Josiah in 1824 and 1825; interviewed by Herndon in 1865.

Charles A. Dana
(1819–1897) New Hampshire–born journalist with the *New York Tribune*, and Lincoln's assistant secretary of war from 1863 to 1865; he wrote *Recollections of the Civil War*.

David Davis
(1815–1886) American jurist and Lincoln's friend; elected judge of the Eighth Judicial District in 1848; in 1862 Lincoln appointed him an Associate Justice of the Supreme Court; he resigned from the Court in 1877 to serve a term in the U.S. Senate.

Edward Dicey	(1832–1911) English journalist and editor of the *London Observer* newspaper.
Stephen Arnold Douglas	(1813–1861) Illinois state attorney, state legislator, and U.S. senator. At the time of his debates with Lincoln, he was one of the best-known politicians in America. He was defeated by Lincoln for the presidency.
Frederick Douglass	(1817?–1895) The son of a white man and a slave; became a lecturer and writer after escaping from slavery. Founder and editor of the abolitionist paper *North Star*.
Joseph Gillespie	(1809–1885) Met Lincoln during the Black Hawk War; member of the Illinois legislature; later a judge. Helped found the Republican Party of Illinois.
Horace Greeley	(1811–1872) American journalist and political leader, he founded the *New York Tribune* and had a major influence on popular thought in the North during and after the Civil War.
Nathaniel "Nat" Grigsby	(1811–1890) Boyhood friend and schoolmate of Lincoln in Indiana; visited the President in Washington.
William H. Herndon	(1818–1891) Lincoln's law partner from 1844 to 1860, "Billy" Herndon served as mayor of Springfield for one term. A devoted friend and admirer of Lincoln, Herndon was the author of *Herndon's Lincoln: The True Story of a Great Life* with Jesse W. Weik.
John Davis Johnston	(1811–1854) The youngest son of Lincoln's stepmother, Sarah Bush Johnston, and childhood comrade of Lincoln. In financial difficulties throughout his life, he died in Coles County, Illinois, virtually destitute.
William Knox	(1789–1825) Scottish poet, contemporary of Sir Walter Scott. Wrote Lincoln's favorite poem, "Mortality."

Ward Hill Lamon	(1828–1893) Lincoln's close friend and law associate from Danville, Illinois. In Washington, he served as marshal of the District of Columbia and often served as personal guard to the President. He wrote *Life of Abraham Lincoln from his Birth to His Inauguration as President.*
Edward Baker Lincoln	(1846–1849) Lincoln's second-born son, named for one of Lincoln's closest friends, "Eddy" died as a child, after an illness of almost two months.
Mary Todd Lincoln	(1818–1882) Born in Kentucky, she married Lincoln in Springfield in 1842. Highly ambitious and gifted, she was also high-strung and hot-tempered. She suffered from mental illness and died a recluse.
Nancy Hanks Lincoln	(1784–1818) Lincoln's mother. Born in Virginia, she died in Indiana when he was nine years old. We know very little about her. We do know that she was illiterate and signed legal documents with a mark.
Robert Todd Lincoln	(1843–1926) Lincoln's oldest child. A graduate of Harvard College, he became a successful lawyer and businessman, served as President Garfield's secretary of war, and was present at Garfield's assassination.
Sarah Lincoln	(1807–1828) Abraham Lincoln's sister; married Aaron Grigsby and died in childbirth.
Sarah Bush Johnston Lincoln	(1788–1869) Lincoln's stepmother. He wrote that she was a "good and kind mother" to him. Born in Kentucky, she died in Illinois four years after Lincoln's death.
Thomas Lincoln	(1778–1851) Abraham Lincoln's father. A carpenter and farmer, he moved to Kentucky from Virginia in the 1780s. Grew up without schooling; married to Nancy Hanks in 1806, and, following her death, to Sarah Bush Johnston in 1819.

Thomas Lincoln	(1812–1812) Abraham Lincoln's younger brother; died in infancy.
Thomas "Tad" Lincoln	(1853–1871) Lincoln's youngest son, he was named for Lincoln's father. When Thomas was young, his head seemed too large for his body; hence the nickname "Tad" for tadpole. He became the President's close companion; he had a learning disability and a speech impediment; died of a respiratory illness.
William Wallace "Willie" Lincoln	(1850–1862) Lincoln's third son. Gentle, loving, and studious, his death in the White House crushed the family. His body was exhumed and carried on Lincoln's funeral train to be buried beside his father in Springfield.
Stephen Twigg Logan	(1800–1880) Highly successful Springfield attorney and member of the Illinois legislature, he was Lincoln's second law partner, from 1841 until 1844. Logan and Lincoln remained on friendly terms until Lincoln's death.
Lindley Murray	(1745–1826) Scottish-American lawyer and grammarian, and called the "Father of English Grammar," Murray wrote schoolbooks that Lincoln read, including *Grammar of the English Language, English Reader,* and *English Spelling Book.*
J. G. Randall	(1891–1953) Influential Lincoln scholar, author, and historian at the University of Illinois.
Robert S. Rantoul	(1832–1922) Massachusetts attorney and contemporary of Lincoln. His recollections were published in the proceedings of the Massachusetts Historical Society in 1909.
Henry J. Raymond	(1820–1869) Founding editor of the *New York Times.*
Robert Brannon Rutledge	(1819–1881) Brother of Ann Rutledge. Became acquainted with Lincoln in New Salem.
Joshua Frye Speed	(1814–1882) Lincoln's closest Springfield

friend, he was born in Kentucky. Returned to Kentucky in 1841; became wealthy through real estate investments. During Civil War, helped smuggle arms to Kentuckians loyal to the Union.

Harriet Beecher Stowe (1811–1896) American writer, daughter of Lyman Beecher, and sister of Henry Ward Beecher—both influential clergymen. An ardent abolitionist, her best-known book is *Uncle Tom's Cabin.*

Leonard Swett (1825–1889) Bloomington, Illinois, lawyer who became Lincoln's friend in 1848; served him as an adviser and political lieutenant.

SOURCES OF THE LINCOLN QUOTATIONS

		As a peace-maker . . . (Fehrenbacher, p. 81)
73	Compassion	On the whole . . . (Hertz, 1938, p. 327)
		I could not . . . (Wilson, 1945, p. 20)
		This is Friday . . . (Hertz, 1986, pp. 516, 517)
75	Trust	I expect the people . . . (Fehrenbacher andFehren-bacher, p. 254)
		Why should there not be . . . (Fehrenbacher, p. 292)
		No hours . . . (Fehrenbacher and Fehrenbacher, p. 194)
77	Achievement	The way for a young man . . . (Hertz, 1986, p. 73)
		The prudent, penniless beginner . . . (Fehren-bacher, p. 234)
		I happen temporarily to occupy . . . (Fehren-bacher, p. 431)
79	Citizenship	Let every American . . . (Fehrenbacher, p. 17)
		Reason, cold, calculating . . . (Fehrenbacher, p. 21)
		Let reverence for the laws . . . (Fehrenbacher, p. 17)
81	Democracy	Government of the people . . . (Basler, VII, p. 23)
		We proposed . . . (Basler, II, p. 222)
83	Patriotism	While pretending no indifference . . . (Basler, II, p. 547)
		How hard . . . (Donald, p. 162)
		I shall be most happy . . . (Fehrenbacher, p. 280)
85	Tolerance	This good earth . . . (Basler, IV, p. 20)
		Our progress . . . (Fehrenbacher, pp. 105–106)
87	Idealism	Something in that Declaration . . . (Fehrenbacher, p. 282)
		I shall do nothing . . . (Basler, V, p. 346)
89	Self-Reliance	Forget that you have anyone . . . (Woldman, p.102)
		I may not rule . . . (Herndon and Weik, III, p. 513)
		I must myself be the judge . . . (Basler, VII, p. 439)
91	Piety	I have so many evidences . . . (Temple, p. 216)
		The will of God prevails . . . (Fehrenbacher, p. 344)

REFERENCES CITED AND RECOMMENDED READING

Abraham Lincoln Association, *Bulletins and Journals.* Old State Capitol, Springfield, Illinois 62701.

Angle, Paul M. *The Lincoln Reader.* New Brunswick, N.J.: Rutgers University Press, 1947.

Basler, Roy P. *The Collected Works of Abraham Lincoln.* New Brunswick, N.J.: Rutgers University Press/The Abraham Lincoln Association, 1953.

Boritt, S. Gabor, ed. *The Historian's Lincoln: Pseudohistory, Psychohistory, and History.* Urbana: University of Illinois Press, 1988.

————. *Of the People, By the People, For the People, and Other Quotations from Abraham Lincoln.* New York: Columbia University Press, 1996.

Burlingame, Michael. *The Inner World of Abraham Lincoln.* Urbana: University of Illinois Press, 1994.

————. *An Oral History of Abraham Lincoln: John G. Nicolay's Interviews and Essays.* Carbondale and Edwardsville: Southern Illinois University Press, 1996.

Carpenter, F. B. *Six Months at the White House with Abraham Lincoln* (1866). Reprinted as *The Inner Life of Abraham Lincoln: Six Months at the White House.* Lincoln: University of Nebraska Press, 1995.

Cuomo, Mario M., and Harold Holzer, eds. *Lincoln on Democracy.* New York: HarperCollins, 1990.

Current, Richard N. *The Lincoln Nobody Knows.* New York: Hill & Wang, 1958.

Dana, Charles A. *Recollections of the Civil War.* New York: D. Appleton & Co., 1898.

Dennett, Tyler, ed. *Lincoln and the Civil War in the Diaries and Letters of John Hay.* New York: Dodd, Mead, 1939 (Da Capo Paperback).

Donald, David Herbert. *Lincoln.* New York: Simon & Schuster, 1995.

Fehrenbacher, Don E. *Lincoln: Selected Speeches and Writings.* New York: Vintage Books/Library of America, 1992.

Fehrenbacher, Don E., and Virginia Fehrenbacher. *Recollected Words of Abraham Lincoln.* Stanford, Calif.: Stanford University Press, 1996.

Foote, Shelby. *The Civil War: A Narrative. Vol. I, Fort Sumter to Perryville.* New York: Random House, 1958.

————. *The Civil War: A Narrative. Vol. II, Fredericksburg to Meridian.* New York: Random House, 1963.

————. *The Civil War: A Narrative. Vol. III, Red River to Appomattox.* New York: Random House, 1974.

Herndon, William H., and Jesse William Weik. *Herndon's Lincoln: The True Story of a Great Life.* Springfield, Ill.: Herndon's Lincoln Publishing Co., 1888.

Hertz, Emanuel, ed. *The Hidden Lincoln: From the Letters and Papers of William H. Herndon.* New York: Viking Press, 1938.

————. *Lincoln Talks: An Oral Biography.* New York: Bramhall House, 1986.

Kerner, Fred. *A Treasury of Lincoln Quotations.* Chicago: Abraham Lincoln Book Shop, 1996.

Kunhardt, Philip B., Philip B. Kunhardt III, and Peter W. Kunhardt. *Lincoln. An Illustrated Biography.* New York: Knopf, 1992.

Lamon, Ward Hill. *Recollections of Abraham Lincoln. 1847–1865.* Lincoln: University of Nebraska Press, 1994.

McClure, J. B. ed. *Anecdotes of Abraham Lincoln and Lincoln's Stories.* Chicago: Rhodes & McClure Publishing Co., 1889.

Mitgang, Herbert, ed. *Abraham Lincoln: A Press Portrait.* Athens: University of Georgia Press, 1989.

Neely, Mark E. *The Abraham Lincoln Encyclopedia.* New York: McGraw-Hill, 1982.

Nevins, Allan. *The War for the Union. Vol. III, The Organized War 1863–1864.* New York: Scribner, 1971.

Newman, Ralph G., ed., *Lincoln for the Ages.* Garden City, New York: Doubleday, 1960.

Nicolay, Helen. *Personal Traits of Abraham Lincoln.* New York: Century Co., 1912.

Nicolay, John G., and John Hay. *Abraham Lincoln: A History.* New York: Century Co., 1890.

Oates, Stephen B. *With Malice Toward None: The Life of Abraham Lincoln.* New York: Mentor, 1977.

―――――. *Abraham Lincoln: The Man Behind the Myths*. New York: Harper & Row, 1984.

Paludan, Phillip Shaw. *The Presidency of Abraham Lincoln*. Lawrence: University Press of Kansas, 1994.

Plowden, David. *Lincoln and His America 1809–1865*. New York: Viking Press, 1970.

Randall, J. G. *Midstream: Lincoln the President*. New York: Dodd, Mead, 1953.

―――――. *Mr. Lincoln*. Edited by Richard N. Current. New York: Dodd, Mead, 1957.

Rice, Allen Thorndike, ed. *Reminiscences of Abraham Lincoln by Distinguished Men of His Time*. New York: North American Review, 1888.

Rothschild, Alonzo. *Lincoln: Master of Men*. Boston: Houghton, Mifflin & Co., 1906.

Sandburg, Carl. *Abraham Lincoln: The Prairie Years and the War Years*. One-volume ed. New York: Galahad Books, 1954.

―――――. *Lincoln Collector: The Story of Oliver R. Barrett's Great Private Collection*. New York: Bonanza Books, 1960.

Stephenson, Nathaniel Wright, ed. and comp. *An Autobiography of Abraham Lincoln*. Indianapolis: Bobbs-Merrill, 1926.

Tarbell, Ida M. *Life of Lincoln*. New York: McClure, Phillips, & Co., 1902.

Temple, Wayne C. *Abraham Lincoln: From Skeptic to Prophet*. Mahomet, Ill.: Mayhaven Publishing, 1995.

Thomas, Benjamin P. *Lincoln's New Salem*. Springfield, Ill.: Abraham Lincoln Association, 1934.

Weik, Jesse W. *The Real Lincoln: A Portrait*. Cambridge, Mass.: Houghton Mifflin, Riverside Press, 1922.

Wills, Garry. *Lincoln at Gettysburg: The Words That Remade America*. New York: Simon & Schuster, 1992.

Wilson, Rufus Rockwell. *Intimate Memories of Lincoln*. Elmira, N.Y.: Primavera Press, 1945.

Woldman, Albert A. *Lawyer Lincoln*. 1936. Reprint, New York: Carroll & Graf, 1994.

Zall, P. M., ed. *Abe Lincoln Laughing: Humorous Anecdotes from Original Sources By and About Abraham Lincoln*. Berkeley: University of California Press, 1982.

ACKNOWLEDGMENTS

Gloria, my daughter, was the first person to suggest that I produce a book of quotations, focusing on Lincoln as a high achiever. The evolution of the project from a book of free-standing quotes to its present form is the result of encouragement from my daughter Sharon, who read it, critiqued it, and steadfastly believed it would be a success, and my daughter Katrina and her husband Jeff, who read the early drafts and offered many useful suggestions. I have shamelessly taken advantage of acquaintances and friends—John E. Angle, Terry Brock, June Cline, John Patrick Dolan, Ivory Dorsey, Kay DuPont, Ken Futch, Bob Gibson, Alastair Hamilton, Teri Kabachnick, Austin McGonigle, Sterling Nelson, Sandra Painton, Terry Paulson, Stephen Preas, Taylor Rosenberg, David Ryback, Karen Shepherd, Terry Vanderwerff, and Richard Weylman—with so many requests for feedback that I'm surprised they still return my calls. My wonderful assistants— Michelle Reisweber and Leah Perry—have responded to every request cheerfully and professionally. The fabulous wordsmith Toni Boyle took a rough manuscript and produced a document that was good enough to interest Simon & Schuster. She was kind enough to call it "a little jewel," which, whether true or not, helped me more than she knows. My thanks to Lois McDonald, who put in many hours verifying the manuscript, and to Warren Bennis, the renowned authority on leadership and management, who read the manuscript and offered valuable comments. I owe a great debt to the following Lincoln scholars: Mr. Kim M. Bauer, coeditor of the *Journal of the Abraham Lincoln Association;* Gabor Boritt, head of the Civil War Institute at Gettysburg College; Harold Holzer, vice president for communications at the Metropolitan Museum of Art; John Sellers, Lincoln curator of the U.S. Library of Congress; Michael Burlingame, author of *The Inner World of*

Abraham Lincoln; and Daniel Weinberg, owner of the Abraham Lincoln Book Shop in Chicago. To Fred Hills, great editor at Simon & Schuster, and his fabulous assistant editor Hilary Black, for believing in the project, offering continuing support and enthusiasm, and for making the book different and much better than I thought it would be—my heartfelt thanks.

ABOUT THE AUTHOR

Charles Casnel

Dr. Griessman is an internationally known author and professional speaker on high achievers and peak performance, time management, and trends in society. He has conducted exclusive interviews with many of this century's most celebrated people, including U.S. presidents, famous entertainers, sports figures, artists, and political and business leaders. He often appears on TV and radio, and his award-winning presentations have aired on WCNN and on TBS. The author of seven books and research monographs, plus articles for newspapers and magazines in the United States and abroad, he has written a one-man play on Abraham Lincoln. As Lincoln, Griessman has performed twice at historic Ford's Theatre, at the Lincoln Memorial, and at numerous conventions, annual meetings, schools, and universities.

Griessman has taught at the College of William and Mary, North Carolina State University, Auburn University, Tuskegee University, Georgia Tech, and at the University of Islamabad in Pakistan, where he was a Fulbright professor. He has been a visiting researcher at universities in Peru and Australia. He is past president of the Georgia Chapter of the National Speakers Association, and is a fellow of the American Anthropological Association.

If you are interested in a Lincoln portrayal for your organization or Gene Griessman's books and cassettes on Lincoln and other high achievers, contact Griessman & Associates, Inc. Tel: 310-230-8971, or 800-749-GOAL (4625). Fax: 310-230-9851. E-mail: abe@mindspring.com. Or visit the achievement webpage: http://www.presidentlincoln.com